Social Capital and Mental Health

Social Capital and Mental Health

*Edited by Kwame McKenzie
and Trudy Harpham*

Foreword by Richard Wilkinson

Jessica Kingsley Publishers
London and Philadelphia

First published in 2006
by Jessica Kingsley Publishers
116 Pentonville Road
London N1 9JB, UK
and
400 Market Street, Suite 400
Philadelphia, PA 19106, USA

www.jkp.com

Library of Congress Cataloging in Publication Data
Social capital and mental health / edited by Kwame McKenzie and Trudy Harpham ; foreword by Richard Wilkinson.
    p. cm.
Includes bibliographical references and index.
ISBN-13: 978-1-84310-355-4 (pbk.)
ISBN-10: 1-84310-355-9 (pbk.)
    1. Mental health--Social aspects. 2. Mental illness--Social aspects. 3. Social capital (Sociology) I. McKenzie, Kwame. II. Harpham, Trudy.
    RA790.5.S56 2006
    362.2--dc22

                                                        2005036040

British Library Cataloguing in Publication Data
A CIP catalogue record for this book is available from the British Library

ISBN-13: 978 1 84310 355 4
ISBN-10: 1 84310 355 9

Printed and bound in Great Britain by
Athenaeum Press, Gateshead, Tyne and Wear

Contents

Acknowledgements

Dr Kwame McKenzie would like to thank Bruce, Ichiro and Tom for introducing him to social capital; Professor Arthur Kleinman for supporting his work in the Department of Social Medicine at Harvard; Professor Robin Murray and Professor Jim van Os for their continued support and encouragement; the Harkness Fellowship programme of the Commonwealth Fund of New York; The Department of Mental Health Sciences at University College London and Natasha, without whom this book could not have been completed.

Foreword

This ambitious book does us the uncomfortable service of showing us how much we have yet to understand. By studying social capital and mental health in radically different contexts – from Alabama to Colombia, from Lusaka to London – we see how effects depend on the context.

The nature of social relations must have major implications for mental health, and it would be wonderful if we knew how to guide societies towards healthier models, but nothing turns out so simply. No doubt partly as a result of the different levels of economic development plus different racial divides and ethnic mixes, what appear to be the same kinds of social phenomenon turn out, in the different contexts covered in this book, to have different effects.

People have often approached social capital as if more social interaction must mean better, forgetting that not all social links reflect a sense of inclusion, belonging or control. Some are vehicles for conflict, tension and anxiety. Bonding within some groups may be a reflection of exclusion from others. And some campaigning community groups may, like trade unions, exist as defences against particular injustices. In each case, the benefits of association may not be strong enough to overcome or counterbalance the negatives to which they may have been reactions.

We have known for some time that just as good social relations – friendship, good marriages, social support – are beneficial to health, so bad relationships – 'negative' relations, hostility, etc. – are bad for health. It is the same at the societal or community level: places in which people are more involved with each other enjoy better mental health but must depend partly on what brings them together – on the divisions and struggles to which they might be responses.

Too often we start research on social capital with definitions, as if our task was simply to define what we are talking about and go out and measure it. But defining something implies that we already know a lot about it. Perhaps social capital is more like a strange animal whose tracks we sometimes find but that rarely shows itself in the light of day. And if we could see it clearly, would we find that the things we call bridging, bonding, cognitive and vertical or horizontal social capital are all parts of the same beast or members of the same herd, or are they separate animals that roam around quite independently of each other? If we discover a new creature, we do not start by defining it before we even know

7

whether it has fur or feathers; instead, we examine it carefully to see what its real characteristics are.

We have an idea that there are important differences in the quality of the social fabric in different societies – something about the way people relate to each other, something that perhaps makes some societies work better than others. But are there just endless variations – different kinds of difference – in the social fabric, or are there a few underlying dimensions that influence everything else? If we were to look at a lot of different societies, would we find bridging and bonding social capital moved together, or would we find one was strong where the other was weak? Are vertical and horizontal capital part of something bigger, or are they unrelated features of social reality? Do better family relations go with stronger bridging capital, or is the real picture one in which weak bridging capital may reflect a lack of confidence in fair and equal treatment in the public sphere, which has sometimes left people reliant on tribal and family loyalties, nepotism and sometimes gangs?

My own working hypothesis is rooted in the widespread perception that inequality is divisive and so socially corrosive. The evidence suggests that there is, indeed, a tendency for social relations to deteriorate in more hierarchical societies as if greater material differences led to increased social distances and more divisive social stratification. Such societies are marked by more violence, lower levels of trust and reduced involvement in community life. At the same time, as the social divisions become bigger and harder to bridge, people may be thrown back on local or family loyalties, implying that bridging and bonding capital may move inversely. Similarly, where the social hierarchy is steeper, the vertical links up and down it are likely to become more difficult.

To test these and other views more rigorously, we need comparable measures from different societies. Simple measures like trust and violence can take us only so far. The review of literature on social capital and mental health contained in Chapter 3 of this book concludes that the difficulty of comparing research findings raises the danger that social capital may be consigned, wrongly, to the 'unproven dustbin of academic ideas'. But it is important not to lose sight of the fact that once access to the material necessities of life is assured, then the quality of our relations with each other is almost certainly the most important determinant of the real subjective quality of our lives. This is what research on social capital is really about.

Richard Wilkinson
Professor of Social Epidemiology,
University of Nottingham

PART 1
Theory and methods

CHAPTER 1

Meanings and uses of social capital in the mental health field

Kwame McKenzie and Trudy Harpham

Introduction: why is social capital important to mental health?

People in some places have better mental health than people in other places. This is not just because of their genetic vulnerability, the physical environment or their socioeconomic status. It also reflects the fabric of society – the way in which communities are set up and people live.

The effect of the structure of society on psychological health has been described for some time. Durkheim's (1951) theories on suicide from the 1890s are notable, and Faris and Dunham (1939) argued in the 1930s that the level of 'disorganisation' within a neighbourhood was a factor that could explain differential rates of mental disorder within the city of Chicago. These are just two examples of the strong tradition of research and innovation in psychiatry concerning the effects of social context on health. However, such theories generally have not led to developments in health policy.

More recently, another way of conceptualizing the social world – social capital – has captured the imagination and has been written into national and international health policies. It is considered an important, some would say pivotal, idea in social policy and health, and all of this has happened despite a relative lack of empirical investigation.

Social capital is a concept explored in disciplines as diverse as criminology, political science and international development. It attempts to describe features of populations such as the level of civic participation, social networks and levels of trust. Such forces shape the quality and quantity of social interactions and the social institutions that underpin society.

If you consider social capital to be a continuous variable, then areas with high social capital may be expected to have a lower rate of illnesses associated with problems of social cohesion compared with areas of low social capital. Indeed, there are reports that areas with high levels of social capital have lower suicide rates, lower all-cause mortality and longer life expectancy.

Some believe that building social capital could decrease health spending and decrease the rates of illness. Their specific interest in mental health is twofold because:

- mental health is one of the top three causes of life-years lost to disability worldwide
- psychological mechanisms are likely to be the way in which social capital affects physical health.

Investigating the social world is complex. Social capital cannot simply be considered as a single continuous variable; areas and people cannot simply be categorized as having high or low social capital; different mental health problems are likely to be linked to different aspects of social capital in different ways, and these links may be direct or through other, poorly defined physical, environmental and societal mechanisms.

But complexity should not be a deterrent given the possible prize. Mental health problems usually can be managed or put into remission but often are not cured. Relapse is common. Where cure is not possible and an illness is chronic, prevention is important. There are wide variations in the rates of mental health problems in different areas and countries. These variations are not due simply to the physical environment or to genes. The social environment is increasingly being implicated and proffered as the cause. Better understanding of the social factors that cause or perpetuate psychological problems is vital if preventive strategies are to be developed to counter these factors. If aspects of social capital prove to be as powerfully associated as has been postulated with even some mental health problems, then it is important that they are studied urgently.

What is social capital?

Before we go further, we need to explore the concept of social capital in more depth. There are a number of competing definitions, some of which are more popularly used than others. Jane Jacobs is claimed to have been the first person to make an explicit reference to the term 'social capital' (Jacobs 1961; Whitley and McKenzie 2005). However, Hanifan (1920) may have described it earlier. Jacobs states: 'Underlying any float of population must be a continuity of people who have forged neighbourhood networks. These networks are a city's irreplaceable social capital.'

Since then, a number of sociologists have tried to define social capital more precisely. With many new concepts, there is a settling-down period during which theorists disagree. Social capital is no different. The most notable disagreement is whether social capital is a property of groups or a property of individuals.

Individual or ecological?

Sociologist Bourdieu's (1986) view of social capital may be considered to reflect an assumption that it is a property of an individual. A person's individual social relationships allow differential access to resources (e.g. healthcare and education) and these relationships define social capital.

Social capital has also been considered as ecological (see McKenzie *et al.* 2002 for review). It would thus relate to groups or areas rather than individuals. Those who follow this definition see social capital as being embodied in relationships between individuals, between groups, and between groups and abstract bodies such as the state.

The problem that many people have with the individual definition is that it is unclear where the existing and well-researched concepts of social support and social networks stop and that of social capital begins. If social capital is simply a measure of an individual's access to social networks or social support, then it is not really a new concept.

There has been a significant body of research into the links between access to social support and illness. Mortality rates for people with few social relationships have been shown to be many times higher than for those with larger social networks. Social support protects against a variety of other illnesses, and low levels of social networks are correlated with an increased risk of accidents, suicide and cardiovascular disease. The lack of a supportive confiding relationship is a risk factor for depression. In addition, Durkheim (1951) found that married men had a lower prevalence of neurosis than single men. Social support is believed to buffer an individual against both chronic and acute stress through the provision of emotional, informational and instrumental support. The socially isolated individual lacks this support and suffers the consequent disadvantages.

If social capital is the property of an individual, then it could be considered to act in a similar manner. Its effects on health could be due to preventing isolation, alienation and lack of access to social support. If this is true, then individual social capital may be a proxy variable for access to the active ingredient – social support and social networks. It would be unclear whether anything is to be gained by employing a new term such as 'social capital' as a proxy variable rather than using the more accurate descriptions of the factors under observation – accessed social support or social networks.

Some researchers who analyse social capital at the individual level extend the concept to include trust, sense of belonging and civic engagement. This goes further than social support and networks, so in these cases social support is not merely being used as a proxy for the older concepts.

The most commonly used definition of social capital in the health sciences originates from the political scientist Robert Putnam. This definition arose out of empirical work on the performance of regional government in Italy and consists of five principal characteristics (Putnam 1993):

- Community networks, voluntary, state, personal networks and density.
- Civic engagement, participation and use of civic networks.
- Local civic identity – sense of belonging, solidarity and equality with local community members.
- Reciprocity and norms of cooperation, a sense of obligation to help others and confidence in return of assistance.
- Trust in the community.

This definition goes beyond conventional social network theory. Local civic identity and trust could be considered descriptions of groups rather than just individuals and thus reflect ecological social capital. The impact of civic identity and trust on health could be considered to have not only individual psychological correlates but also ecological effects. For instance, individuals with both high and low levels of trust could benefit if the community in general had high levels of trust and civic identity and therefore invested in community facilities that everyone had access to. Although an individual's access to community facilities would be important, the actual level of facilities that are available are governed by the overall level of trust in the community rather than the level of trust or civic identity of the individual in question. The overall level of trust and civic identity in a community is the important factor in the provision of infrastructure rather than that of any individual under consideration. It is this general level of trust, identity, fraternity and networks that Putnam identifies.

Despite this, we will see in Chapter 3 that some have constructed measures of social capital and analysed results of studies based on Putnam's view of social capital but at an individual level.

Types of social capital

As interest in the concept has increased, so have attempts to further refine levels and types of social capital.

As with the gross definition of social capital, there is ongoing debate about the accuracy of these subtypes. However, they are important, as they propose that social capital is multidimensional. They also rely, as do most of the hitherto discussed definitions, on a triad of factors that are the essential building blocks of social capital: relationships, norms and trust. These exist between, as well as within, groups and institutions.

We can consider social capital to have at least three dimensions: structural/cognitive, bonding/bridging and horizontal/vertical. Some have individual as well as ecological correlates, while others are difficult to conceptualize at an individual level.

STRUCTURAL AND COGNITIVE SOCIAL CAPITAL

Structural social capital describes the relationships, networks, associations and institutions that link together people and groups. They can, thus, be crudely measured numerically or through an analysis of linkages or network density. For instance, the number of church groups, local societies, Sunday league football teams or volunteer groups in an area and the percentage of people who participate may be considered a measure of structural social capital. Some consider an individual correlate to be individual participation in groups outside the work environment.

Cognitive social capital consists of values, norms, reciprocity, altruism and civic responsibility, sometimes called 'collective moral resources'. Some have measured this by performing surveys of the level of trust in neighbours and civic identity and comparing rates of trust in one area with those in another. At an individual level, one could measure perceptions of community such as sense of belonging and trust.

BONDING AND BRIDGING SOCIAL CAPITAL

Social capital can be considered as bridging (inclusive) or bonding (exclusive). Bonding social capital is inward-focused and characterized by homogeneity, strong norms, loyalty and exclusivity. It is intra-group and relies on strong ties. It can be thought of as the type of social capital that a family unit has or that found in small close-knit migrant groups who need mutual support.

Bridging social capital is outward-focused and links different groups in society. The ties between people are weaker, and some would consider bridging social capital to be more fragile. An individual's social networks reflect that person's bridging social capital.

Bonding social capital can have a negative effect on society as a whole. For example, organized crime groups like the Mafia are often depicted as being closely bonded. In contrast, bridging social capital generally is considered to be a positive thing. It acts as a sociological superglue, binding together groups in the community, and so can facilitate common action.

HORIZONTAL AND VERTICAL SOCIAL CAPITAL

A final dimension by which social capital can be split is horizontal and vertical. Horizontal social capital describes social capital between people in similar strata of society, and vertical social capital describes social capital that provides integration between people in different strata of society.

Essentially, horizontal social capital can be considered to include the bonding social capital, bridging social capital and cognitive and structural social capital that are confined to particular social strata. An example would be bonding social capital within a wealthy family and bridging social capital through exclusive clubs (which link them to similarly rich families) together with all their structural and cognitive correlates.

Vertical social capital can be seen as the degree of integration of groups within a hierarchical society that allows it to influence policy and access justice and resources from those in power. It can be seen as a type of bridging social capital with structural components referring to the organizational integrity, penetration and effectiveness of the state and cognitive elements reflecting group identity (Woolcock 1998).

Refining definitions

Validation and refinement of concepts are normally prerequisites for empirical testing. Otherwise, there can be no certainty that the same phenomenon is under observation in different studies. Similarly, terminological precision is usually a precondition for the building of effective theory.

There is agreement among leading theorists that validation is an urgent priority. Although there is no agreed definition of social capital, most theorists state that trust, networks and norms are its three main components.

Measuring social capital

As would be expected in a growing area with competing theories, there are many different tools available to measure social capital. Although tools are available, however, many have not been validated, and few capture all of the dimensions of social capital. There is less of a problem with producing questionnaires that try to measure individual social capital than with trying to measure group or area social capital. Many studies trying to work ecologically rely on measuring the individual's perception of society and then aggregating individual perceptions to group or area levels. It is unclear how valid this is. It could be argued that instead of questionnaires, which rely on the sum of individual perception, other observational measures of societal structure may be needed.

The number of civic associations has been used, as have measures of community effectiveness and indicators of trust, such as whether local petrol stations demand prepayment before motorists fill their tanks or whether stores allow credit.

But it could also be argued that the sum of individual perceptions in an area or group is more important for community building and the psychological health of the community than actual structures in society.

There are more fundamental questions. If we are measuring context, what context should we measure? What is a community – is it geographical or psychological or functional, e.g. a work or religious community? If it is geographical, then what area size should we measure and who should define it – the community or the policy-makers? Social capital has been measured in a number of different sizes of population and areas, including at US state level, in UK electoral wards and on particular housing estates. Which of these is correct, or should we be using different sizes of area depending on the social context?

The belief that social capital resides primarily in the neighbourhood has been perpetuated in the empirical work. Indeed, in this book, all our country studies are geographical. However, the assumption that communities generally are place-based may be erroneous, and this issue needs further attention. Some sociologists have claimed that modern society is characterized by constant change, with individuals constantly constructing and reconstructing their sense of self (Giddens 1991; Cohen and Wills 1985). This is made possible by the range of choices and lifestyles available in the modern world and leads to a semi-permanent state of dislocation and instability. Place as a factor in the perception of security is considered to have diminished rapidly, due to a combination of globalization, technology, post-modernism and infrastructural developments. The present is marked by greater heterogeneity in terms of demography, behaviour and lifestyle. It is vastly different from the world of self-contained homogeneous and stable neighbourhoods that characterized earlier traditional eras. In this social milieu, non-spatial communities may dwarf the neighbourhood community in importance for individuals. These non-spatial communities have not come under the spotlight in studies of social capital, despite the opportunities offered by multilevel modelling.

For example, a refugee living in a stable neighbourhood of a large city may find support in the city-wide refugee community from the same country far more important than the neighbourhood community. Many faith groups find their faith community more important than their residential community, especially if they are in the minority in their geographical area. Socially excluded groups such as those suffering from mental illness may link with each other through support groups, which increasingly are based on telephone lines and the Internet.

It is an open question as to whether the concepts of social capital developed for spatial communities are applicable in non-spatial communities and what kind of impact it has on community members. There is a need for further research into the nexus between the individual, the neighbourhood community and the non-spatial communities to which they belong. There is also a need to define and refine concepts of community and to determine the appropriate unit of ecological analysis.

Before we get too carried away with the hype about new non-spatial societies, we may want to reflect on the fact that geographically based associative behaviour was present and important in all the studies we report in this book. Moreover, people are likely to continue to belong to a number of different communities, both geographical and non-spatial. The rise of the latter may diminish but not extinguish the importance of the former. Moreover, area-based government and health services are likely to find area-based policy easier to promote.

What is good for one group in society may not be good for another. The possibility of a differential impact of social capital on subgroups is well recognized. All the different dimensions of social capital discussed earlier could vary according to the group in question. For example, relatively immobile groups such as children and elderly people may be more affected by neighbourhood social capital than groups with high relative mobility. Similarly, minority groups or new arrivals to a town may find some strong forms of social capital impenetrable and exclusionary in nature.

Studies aiming to unravel such complex issues require sophisticated methodology based on sound hypotheses. Measurement and methodological issues are of such importance that this book devotes a whole chapter to them.

Social capital for societal change

Refining methodology and measurement is important, but more in-depth exploration of possible associations and mechanisms through which various aspects of social capital may be linked to mental illness is vital if effective policy is to be developed. It could help us to decide what sort of interventions should be developed, where and how they should be targeted, and at what level such policies should be pursued.

For instance, continuing our brief consideration of place, understanding whether any link between aspects of social capital and mental health in a population is group- or area-based will help us decide whether eventual interventions should be aimed at an area or cross-sectionally targeted at a non-spatial target group.

If different impacts of aspects of social capital on mental health are discovered, then this may help decisions to be made about how best policy-makers should proceed. For instance, if research reported that bridging social capital was generally considered useful in improving health in a community, but bonding social capital has a variable association with mental illness, then policy-makers may decide initially to try to facilitate the development of the former.

If vertical social capital was considered more important for mental health than any of the other aspects, then this would argue for a central rather than a local government to act. Vertical aspects of social capital are dependent on the capacities of individual communities but also reliant on communal-state relations (i.e. governance).

A deeper understanding of the links between aspects of social capital and mental health may also help to disentangle aspects of social capital and their outcomes. Collective characteristics such as social capital and neighbourhood are sometimes considered outcome variables in themselves rather than exposure variables. This causes problems, because collective characteristics of neighbourhood, for example, may be due to the historical and geographical development of a city or the housing policies of public authorities. These forces engineer neighbourhoods in a non-random fashion perpetuating, rather than creating, inequalities (Harvey 1973). Where there is choice, areas rich in social capital may attract more people who participate in the community at the expense of other areas. For these reasons, social capital may be an epiphenomenon of wider structural factors rather than a community-based outcome. This needs further exploration before public policy is formed, because the chances of success of any intervention will be lower if factors external to the current community – whether historical, structural or political – are working against it. Attempts at building residential stability and community cohesion to improve mental health in a poor urban area of a high-income country are unlikely to be effective if the general message from the rest of society is that individuals need to get on by getting out.

Social capital, mental health and poverty

Social capital now often appears in the debate on the link between mental health and poverty. The poverty–mental health link is cyclical. The harsh conditions of poverty and associated experiences such as gender-based violence, material deprivation, low education and poor physical health contribute to poor mental health, while the latter impedes productivity, may pose an increased care burden on family members, and leads to increased healthcare costs, thus increasing poverty.

This is true in urban poor areas of high-income countries but is of a different magnitude in low-income countries. In low-income countries, it is increasingly recognized that novel ways are needed to break this cycle based on a fuller understanding of the mechanisms that explain the complex relationship between poverty and mental health; the development of integrated individual, population, community and health service approaches to improving mental health; the application of research outcomes to health and other sector reforms such as social welfare; and the strengthening of the case for investment in mental health in the context of scarce resources and high burden of communicable diseases.

The 'social' appears in the above argument a number of times, in terms of both designing and testing community (as opposed to individual) interventions and recognizing that action for mental health rests not only with the health sector but also with social sectors such as ministries of welfare, education, employment and even engineering (in relation to improving the physical environment).

The ascendance of the 'social' in mental health is often confused or subsumed within the debate about the role of 'place' in mental health, i.e. the contextual effects on mental health that remain above and beyond the compositional (individual) effects on mental health. In this book, we are not dealing with all contextual effects but only social capital. Indeed, sometimes social capital is measured as an individual-level variable and is not aggregated up to examine it as a contextual or ecological factor.

Figure 1.1 separates out the elements of area effects on mental health in order to clarify the role of social capital vis-à-vis other area effects. Note that research does not yet give us many clues as to which of these potential area effects are confounding variables and which are on the causal pathway to mental health (Macintyre *et al.* 2002).

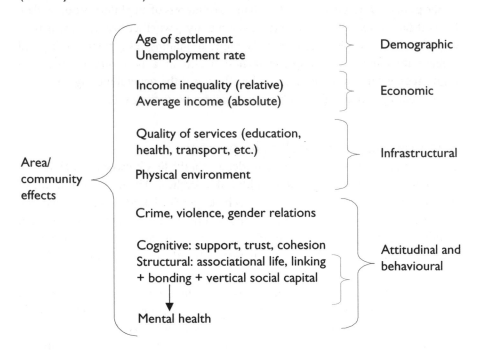

Figure 1.1 The embededness of social capital within area effects on mental health

Methodologically weaker studies of social capital tend to blur the boundaries between these different categories of area effects and, for example, include perceptions of the quality of the physical environment as a component of social capital (Harpham *et al.* 2002; see also Chapter 3). Their measures of social capital tend to be too broad and all-encompassing. We need to move towards a lean and mean definition and measurement of social capital.

There are an increasing number of criticisms of social capital as a concept and as a tool for development. Many of these criticisms suggest that tackling social capital means neglecting the other area effects presented in Figure 1.1 and the wider effects that are not limited to specific areas. For example, a main criticism of social capital involves what Harriss (2002) has famously dubbed its 'depoliticizing' implications. Harriss takes issue with the World Bank's conceptualization of social capital, which he argues not only obscures the importance of macroeconomic structural problems and class politics in poverty reduction debates but also, through a focus on the role of communities, shifts attention away from the state's responsibility for service provision. Emphasizing the fundamental role that power relations can have in contributing to poverty, he further criticizes the World Bank for the absence of a focus on avowedly political associations such as political parties and trade unions and an underlying assumption that 'suggests it is possible to have effective democracy without the inconveniences of contestational politics' (Harriss p.117). As scholars of social movements have also gradually come to realize, 'It is perfectly possible for resource-poor people to have strong social networks but deliver little' (Harriss p.117). In a similar vein, Pearce and Smith (2003, p.8) argue: 'There has been little discussion of the possibility that focusing on what materially and politically disenfranchised communities can do for themselves may be akin to victim blaming at the community level.'

However, most of these criticisms that social capital research ignores structural issues seem to assume that social capital researchers are treating the concept as a narrow magic bullet and suggesting that other factors either do not matter or should not be tackled through public policy. This is not the stance that the editors of this book take. Indeed, the editors are clear that integration of communities in the power structures of a society (i.e. 'vertical social capital') is a vitally important type of social capital that is not measured often. We have an obligation to assess whether social capital has an independent effect above and beyond structural factors like poverty. But most people who use a social model of mental health accept that a variety of actions are needed to improve and protect mental health. Some of the criticisms stem from the way in which social capital has been conceptualized and measured. Including consideration of vertical aspects of social capital helps to emphasize the differences between the social capital literature and governance (interaction between state and civil society) literature.

Building international knowledge

Much of the published discourse and research into social capital and mental health has been in high-income countries. This is despite the fact that much of the original interest in social capital stemmed from international organizations interested in the development of low-income countries. Unfortunately, although there is significant international interest in developing social capital in low-income countries in general, there is much less interest in social capital and mental health. This is worrying, because the important impact of mental health problems in low-income countries is increasingly being documented.

Whether social capital is of international relevance is not in doubt, but it is unclear as to how transferable data and knowledge are between countries. Research has demonstrated how difficult it is to compare work in two developed countries, even though similar tools are used (Drukker *et al.* 2005). Making comparisons between more culturally and economically diverse areas will be challenging. To date, no one has attempted to synthesize the information, experience and knowledge that has been built up from researchers investigating social capital across the globe. Because of this, skills have not been transferred, there has not been balanced international discourse, and the development of the field has been more haphazard than it need be.

Social capital may be a useful tool internationally in the prevention of mental illness and disability. However, we need to better understand how to measure it, how it impacts on mental health and whether the research that predominantly has been in high-income countries is transferable to low-income countries.

In this book, we start this process. We analyse the concept of social capital by presenting qualitative, quantitative and mixed methodologies. We present studies ranging from smaller in-depth work carried out by one researcher to broader large-population surveys. We present studies from high-income and low-income countries spanning the world and move from simple observational studies to an attempt at building social capital and documenting its impact on psychological health.

References

Bourdieu, P. (1986) *Forms of Capital.* New York: Free Press.

Cohen, S., Wills, T.A. (1985) Stress, social support and the buffering hypothesis. *Psychological Bulletin 98,* 310–357.

Drukker, M., Buka, S.A., Kaplan, C., McKenzie, K., van Os, J. (2005) Social capital and young adolescents' perceived health in different sociocultural settings. *Social Science and Medicine 611,* 185–198.

Durkheim, E. (1951) *Suicide.* New York: Free Press.

Faris, R.E.L., Dunham, H.W. (1939) *Mental Disorders in Urban Areas.* Chicago: University of Chicago Press.

Giddens, A. (1991) *Modernity and Self-Identity.* Cambridge: Polity Press.

Hanifan, L. (1920) *The Community Centre Boston.* Boston, MA: Silver Burdett.

Harpham, T., Grant, E., Thomas, E. (2002) Measuring social capital in health surveys: key issues. *Health Policy and Planning 17,* 106–111.

Harriss, J. (2002) *Depoliticizing Development: The World Bank and Social Capital.* London: Anthem Press.

Harvey, D. (1973) *Social Justice and the City.* London: Edward Arnold.

Jacobs, J. (1961) *The Death and Life of Great American Cities.* London: Penguin.

Macintyre, S., Ellaway, A., Cummins, S. (2002) Place effects on health: how can we conceptualise, operationalise and measure them? *Social Science and Medicine 55,* 125–139.

McKenzie, K., Whitley, R., Weich, S. (2002) Social capital and mental illness. *British Journal of Psychiatry 181,* 280–283.

Pearce, N., Smith, D. (2003) Rekindling health care reform: is social capital the key to inequalities in health? *American Journal of Public Health 93,* 122–129.

Putnam, R. (1993) *Making Democracy Work: Civic Traditions in Modern Italy.* Princeton, NJ: Princeton University Press.

Whitley, R., McKenzie, K. (2005) Social capital and psychiatry: review of the literature. *Harvard Review of Psychiatry 13,* 71–84.

Woolcock, M. (1998) Social capital and economic development: towards a theoretical synthesis and policy framework. *Theory and Society 2,* 151–208.

CHAPTER 2

Social risk, mental health and social capital

Kwame McKenzie

Three linked questions dominate the debate on social capital and mental health:

- Can social capital prevent mental illness?
- Can lack of social capital cause mental illness?
- Does the level and/or type of social capital in an area have an impact on the rate of mental illness?

In order to answer these questions we need to consider the association between social capital and mental illness and whether social capital can be considered causative. For ease, we will consider social capital initially as a single entity, although it is clear that there are problems with considering it as such. As associations between social capital and mental illness are discussed in Part 2 of this book, here we will discuss mainly causation and risk.

It is perhaps best to first note that causes for most illnesses are illusive. Linking one complex social theory – social capital – to another – mental illness – could be considered folly. But such folly is the purpose of this chapter and is important for policy-makers.

This chapter will start by retracing some simple causation concepts, move on to causation in mental health, and finally offer some models for beginning to think about the possible impact of social capital on mental health.

Causation

Before an exposure can be considered to cause an illness, there are a number of issues that need to be considered. These can be reduced to four tests.

First, there needs to be an association or correlation between the exposure and the illness. We will see later in this book that associations between different aspects of social capital and a variety of mental illnesses have been demonstrated. The most comprehensive review of the literature to date also supports this assertion (De Silva *et al.* 2005).

Second, there needs to be a temporal sequence of events. The proposed cause has to come before the disease. This is often problematic throughout medicine, and especially in mental illness, because many disorders have a long lag time between exposure and the development of problems (Gelder *et al.* 2004). Longitudinal research investigating social capital and mental health is methodologically challenging, expensive and, not surprisingly, rare. That which has been undertaken is inconclusive (De Silva *et al.* 2005).

Third, there needs to be no other explanatory variable that affects both the cause and the outcome and that could explain the association. Causation theories in mental illness get into difficulty here. Most mental illnesses are complex multifactorial problems where there are a number of other possible explanatory variables. This is partly because many illnesses are caused by a number of factors acting directly on a person or their social and behavioural environment, which increases or decreases risk. It is also because aetiological factors in many illnesses act indirectly through complex intervening mechanisms to produce their effects (Gelder *et al.* 2004).

Given this complexity, most epidemiological studies in mental illness attempt not to demonstrate the cause of an illness but to identify risk or preventive factors or other factors that may help predict an illness or its outcome. The aim is not to find a single cause but to work out what proportion of the rate of an illness or risk of an illness can be explained by its association with the 'causative' variable (Gelder *et al.* 2004).

This is an important area where people misunderstand epidemiological research into mental health problems. While there are many who want to know what the cause of an illness is so that they can prevent it, epidemiological researchers often investigate associations and offer information on what proportion of the risk or rate of an illness may be explained by a particular exposure.

Epidemiological research into social capital to date has rarely attempted to answer the question of whether social capital causes mental illness. Rather, it has aimed to determine whether social capital is associated with mental illness and the size of the association.

We will see in the second part of this book that increasing methodological sophistication aims to control for other possible causes and to assess the size of any association between social capital and mental illness.

The fourth test for causality is that there needs to be a plausible mechanism by which the exposure can lead to the illness. Or, in other words, how could differing rates of social capital lead to mental illness? Before we start to consider this challenge, we need to consider aetiological theories of mental illness.

Aetiology and mental illness

In this book, we use the terms 'mental health', 'mental illness' and 'mental health problems'. The term 'mental health' is considered to refer to an unimpeded sense of psychological and functional wellbeing. The term 'mental illness' refers to specific mental disorders as defined and classified by the World Health Organization's (WHO) *International Classification of Diseases* system or the USA's *Diagnostic and Statistical Manual of Mental Disorders*. The term 'mental health problems' refers to symptoms of psychological difficulties; these include diagnosable mental illnesses and subclinical states.

In practice, social capital studies do not tend to measure mental health. They tend to measure mental health problems as mental illness, as symptoms of psychological distress, which indicate that a mental illness may be present, or as symptoms or behaviours that are considered aberrant but do not warrant a diagnosis, such as binge drinking (see Chapter 3).

According to available classification systems, there are many different types of mental illness. They vary in their symptoms, causes and prognosis as well as in their incidence and prevalence. Using mental health or mental illness as a collective term is problematic because of this heterogeneity. In this book, we will try to be as specific as possible, but in the more general chapters, including this one, we will often consider mental health problems as a single collective group of psychological manifestations of distress. This will aid the development of our initial thinking but subsequently will need refinement.

There is clear evidence for the importance of biological factors in the development of many mental illnesses, but there is also clear evidence for the importance of environmental, societal and behavioural factors. Even in the minority of illnesses where there is a clear unequivocal biological aetiology (for instance, when a genetic abnormality has been demonstrated to be necessary for the development of an illness), the onset, severity and course of the illness may be affected by the social world (Gelder *et al.* 2004).

Illnesses vary in the proportion of the risk of developing them that can be attributed to social factors.

Models of development of mental illness

Using a simplified model of the development of mental health problems, individuals can be considered to be in psychological balance most of the time. There are variations in their psychological state, but these are not problematic.

Figure 2.1 presents a pathway of an individual from this state of balance through to eventual contact with mental health services. Movement up or down the pathway depends on how an individual's risk factors and protective factors operate. Starting at 'balance', if the risk factors outweigh the protective factors, then the person may become distressed. Becoming distressed leads the person to call on other protective factors to try to move them back to balance.

However, if the risk factors still outweigh the protective factors, there is further progression down, perhaps, to the development of regular symptoms. These symptoms lead to a further marshalling of coping resources and structures to try to deal with the emerging problem, and so on.

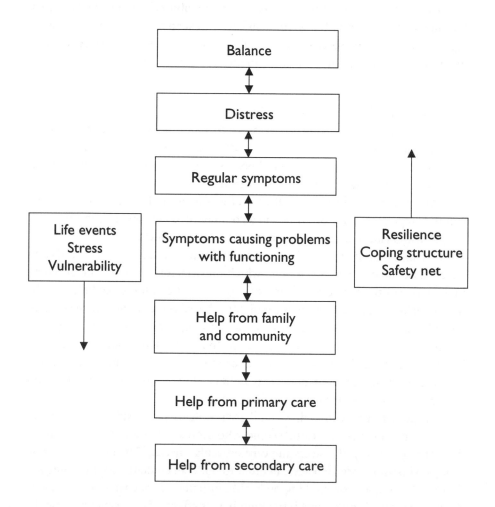

Figure 2.1 Pathway from psychological balance to mental health service use

The peculiar vulnerability of the individual and their community, and the risk factors that are promoting distress, define which of the many mental illnesses the individual ends up suffering from.

A non-exhaustive list of risk factors would include personal vulnerability (for instance, genetic susceptibility, personality, and factors in the individual's upbringing that make them prone to mental illness), acute life events and chronic stress. Protective factors include resilience, social safety nets and coping resources.

Risk factors and protective factors are interrelated. For instance, chronic social stresses such as racism may make some individuals in a group more prone to illness but may also increase the resilience of others. Resources are not static: the use of social support networks predicts their more robust development. However, for the purposes of simplifying our model, we can keep resources and risk factors separate. In the final analysis, it is the balance of risk and protective factors that predicts an individual's progress through increasing levels of distress.

Ecological and individual risk factors

Both ecological and individual processes can be depicted by the model, even though these processes work at different levels. Individual processes work directly on a person, while ecological processes change the group environment and the context in which risk factors operate.

For the ecological level, the labels on the model can be changed so that the pathway represents rates of distress in a community or group, the proportion of people with symptoms, and incidence rates or treated incidence.

It is important to differentiate between individual and ecological social capital, because the mechanisms through which these factors work will be different. Indeed, one of the criticisms of the work to date is that it too often falls into the trap of making inferences about the individual based on ecological analyses (ecological fallacy) or making inferences about the community based on analyses at an individual level (atomistic fallacy) (Diez-Roux 1998). It is not that these two levels are not linked but that there does need to be clarity in the investigation, the use of research and the subsequent generation of hypotheses for the mechanisms considered to be responsible for any association.

It is perhaps easier to understand these problems by considering the case of smoking and premature death. People who smoke have an increased risk of developing a variety of cancers and cardiovascular disease. The rates of illness in groups who smoke are increased. In order to build an evidence-based strategy to decrease the impacts of smoking on health, initially we may want to investigate the mechanisms through which smoking has its effects. The mechanisms can be interrogated in a number of ways and at a number of levels. For instance:

- *Molecular level*: how do nicotine and tar affect the contents of a cell?
- *Metabolic level*: how do cell death and disruption affect other bodily systems?
- *Individual level*: why does the individual smoke, why can the individual not stop smoking, and what can the individual do to decrease the risk caused by smoking?
- *Group level*: why do certain social groups smoke more than others?
- *Societal level*: why do some societies smoke more than others, and what can be done legislatively to decrease the rate of harm from smoking?

All of these investigations have the same aim – to investigate the mechanisms linking smoking and illness – but the analytical tools needed and the theory and scientific rules at each level are different, as are the inferences that can be made from the research. Using the tools and methodology of molecular biology to investigate societal-level factors is unlikely to work very well. Similarly, we are unlikely to understand an individual's metabolic pathophysiology by using systems theory of group dynamics. Investigating smoking legislation and tariffs may give an indication of why the rate of smoking is higher in one country than another; for example, it may give information on why there are consequent increases in, for instance, cardiovascular illness in one area or another. However, such investigation does not give information on an individual's risk of harm if he or she is a smoker or why one person smokes and another does not.

This explanation is clear if we consider smoking, but it is surprising how often authors of excellent ecological epidemiological work investigating social capital attempt to explain their findings in terms of individual risk and the actions of individuals instead of considering group effects and group risk.

Complexity in mental illness aetiology

There is an added level of complexity. For mental illnesses with completely biological aetiologies, such as purely genetic illnesses, some could argue that no level of social or societal risk factors will be important. This would be of more concern if these illnesses formed the majority rather than a tiny minority of mental illnesses. Indeed, it is arguable whether there is really any illness that is completely biological in its aetiology.

Individual risk factors for mental illness include:

- low birth weight
- parent with a mental illness
- physical illness

- substance misuse
- lower educational and employment levels
- low autonomy in the workplace
- urban birth and residence
- certain life events, e.g. victim of violence.

Individual protective factors for mental illness include:

- social support
- education/higher social position
- marriage (for men)
- autonomy at work.

Factors that increase the rate of mental illness in a community include:

- disorganization
- unpredictability
- low trust, high anxiety and high vigilance
- high migration rates
- high crime rates
- low safety-net provision.

Community risk-lowering factors include:

- cohesiveness/predictability
- low crime rates
- low income inequality
- high safety-net provision
- high investment in human capital.

Could social capital cause or prevent mental illness?

The model shown in Figure 2.1 suggests that mental disorders arise from an interplay between risk factors and protective factors working on a person or group with biological, psychobehavioural and social vulnerabilities in a societal context.

The possible mechanisms through which social capital is considered to have an impact on the rates of mental illness have not been researched empirically. However, it is possible to use our knowledge of how different types of social capital impact on community function in order to build speculative models for their possible associations with mental health (for review, see Cullen and Whiteford 2001).

Bonding and bridging social capital and mental health

Civic associations and groups glue society together. They offer a number of different access points so that individuals and families can be involved in society and meet each other. These allow the development of civic identity and enhance social status.

The weak social ties created by voluntary associations socially cohere communities. They prevent individuals from becoming isolated and encourage active engagement within the community. They also offer places where conflicts can be understood and managed. The skills acquired through being involved in civil society are important both on a horizontal level and vertically when negotiating with organisations. Moreover, being able to identify and articulate the needs of a constituency is a persuasive political position.

Communities with high levels of bridging social capital not only may manage conflict better but also the skills developed may allow them to apply pressure on government in order to obtain resources.

Areas with higher levels of social efficacy may be better at protecting their structural social capital such as social and health services. They may be more able to organize to fight budget cuts, such as the closure of a school or a hospital. They may be more able to unite to form pressure groups that produce appropriate social organizations that can be accessed easily. In times of crisis, for instance during war or drought, such areas are more able to unite in order to protect and support their residents.

Areas low in bonding and bridging social capital may have fractured social relations. A relative absence of societal safety nets could be considered likely due to low levels of willingness to invest. These areas would be less able to offer the types of social support that could act as a buffer to prevent the progression of life's challenges into mental illness. Similarly, such areas may be less able to provide support, which may aid restitution, to the families and carers of people with mental illness.

The ties between individuals in areas are also used to transmit knowledge. In areas with higher levels of bonding and bridging social capital, communication is easier. Positive health messages may thus be easier to promote.

If these bonded and bridged groups have higher levels of social control, then policing of health norms and correction of deviant health behaviours such as smoking, underage sex and drug misuse may be facilitated.

Variations in the availability of psychosocial resources at the community level may help to explain the anomalous finding that socially isolated individuals residing in more cohesive communities do not appear to suffer the same ill-health consequences as those living in less cohesive communities (Kawachi and Berkman 2000).

Bridging social capital trust and cognitive social capital

The ties that link communities may also facilitate the development of trust. Association membership and civic trust are highly correlated. Per capita group membership, for instance, in the USA has been shown to be correlated inversely with age-adjusted all-cause mortality (Kawachi *et al.* 1997). Density of civic association membership similarly is a predictor of death from coronary heart disease, malignant neoplasm and infant mortality (Cullen and Whiteford 2001; Kawachi and Berkman 2000).

Levels of distrust are correlated significantly with age-adjusted mortality rates. Apart from the potentially injurious effects and anxiety produced by having to continually reassess one's environment in a low-trust community, higher levels of physical illness lead to higher levels of mental illness as people try to cope psychologically.

The provision of health services and levels of education in an area may be linked to the level of investment in human capital – higher investment could be expected in areas with high trust and high levels of social cohesiveness. Health service provision would be expected to influence the prevalence of mental illness.

From a different perspective, but with the same outcome, the level of social capital may influence government performance, such as the government's capacity to develop and implement policy. According to Lavis and Stoddart (1999):

> Social capital could affect this capacity by, for example, affecting support for re-distributive policies or for universal health-care insurance, both of which could represent core government objectives. A government operating in a jurisdiction with a low level of social capital may lack electoral support for such interventions and so could not proceed with them at least not without significant political risk.

Areas with low levels of investment in infrastructure may accentuate disability and impairment, for instance by poor maintenance of streets and transport systems. There is evidence that disability and impairment, especially in older people, is a direct risk factor for the aetiology and maintenance of depression (Prince *et al.* 1997).

Moreover, social disorganization, defined as the 'inability of a community structure to realize the common values of its residents and maintain effective social controls', correlates to rates of suicide and crime (Sampson and Groves 1989).

Poorer informal community surveillance and non-enforcement of conventional norms by the authorities and the civil population could lead to increased rates of crime, substance abuse and domestic violence, in turn increasing the incidence of mental illness. With regard to the origins of crime, residents of cohesive communities may be better able to control the youth behaviours that set the context for gang violence (Kawachi and Berkman 2000).

However, it would be wrong to think that social capital will necessarily be good for mental health. Highly bonded communities may have little tolerance for people with psychological difficulties. Rather than help these people, highly bonded communities may seek to exclude them: they may believe that such people may promote negative health norms and may be burdensome (McKenzie *et al.* 2002; Whitley and McKenzie 2005).

Social capital and mental health – mechanisms

But how does this help us to answer the question about whether social capital causes mental illness?

We will now attempt to bring together some of these ideas and findings into a working, if only speculative, general model. The aim is not to provide definitive mechanisms by which social capital causes mental illness but to offer some examples of how we may start to think about the links between social capital and mental illness in order to satisfy the fourth test for causation – a plausible mechanism.

For the first model, we consider social capital as a single entity and mental illness as a single entity (see Figure 2.2). From the available evidence, areas with low social capital are characterized by a number of factors that have an impact on the rate of the population with a balanced psychological state in the community.

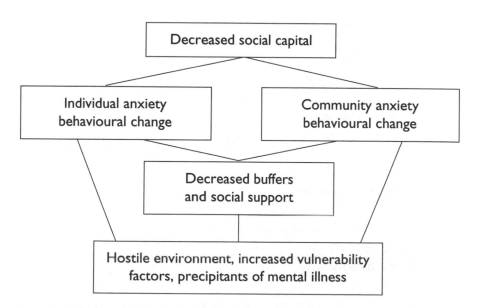

Figure 2.2 Mechanism through which decreased social capital leads to a hostile environment

These include factors such as life events, for instance due to crime. Meanwhile, factors that help bring people back to balance, such as safety-net provision and social support, could be expected to be decreased. The environment would, therefore, be considered as generally more psychologically toxic. If there is stress due to factors in the environment over which people may not have control and there is less help to deal with it, then it is conceivable that there would be increased rates of anxiety in the community. It is also conceivable that this will be played out at a community level as lower levels of trust (social anxiety). The anxiety leads to cognitive and behavioural changes at both a community and an individual level. Lower levels of trust at a community level decrease the likelihood of the population wanting to support investment in infrastructure, and increased levels of anxiety at an individual level decrease the person's capacity to be part of a community and perform their family duties. It may lead to difficulties from an early age with developing the psychological mechanisms to support others and to deal with problems. This amplifies the impact of the hostile environment. The ability of a community to stop people progressing from distress to illness is decreased, and hence the rate of mental illness in a community is increased.

A less abstract model could be that shown in Figure 2.3. Informal and formal social control are considered by some to be forms of social capital. Indeed, they

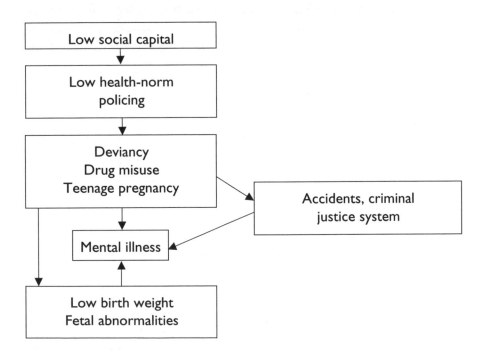

Figure 2.3 An example of a mechanism through which low social control could lead to increased incidence of mental illness

are measured by some of the better studies. Lower levels of such social control have been associated with increased rates of various form of deviancy. Health norms such as avoiding drugs of misuse and teenage pregnancy are less well enforced. Because of this, one would expect higher levels of addiction, teenage pregnancy and involvement with the criminal justice system. These are all risk factors for mental illness. In addition, higher rates of substance misuse and teenage pregnancy would predict increased rates of fetal abnormalities and lower-birth-weight babies. Low-birth-weight babies and babies with abnormalities are at increased risk of mental illness when they grow up. Moreover, the mothers of children with abnormalities are also at increased risk of suffering from postpartum mental illness. The model, would, therefore predict that lower levels of social capital lead to a cascade that increases the rate of mental illness.

Figure 2.4 develops ideas for a link between social capital and mental illness based on governmental performance and the lack of vertical integration of communities into decision-making. Areas low in social efficacy may be more politically marginalized. Add to this lower vertical social capital, and it is not hard to imagine that it may be difficult for such communities to produce an adequate

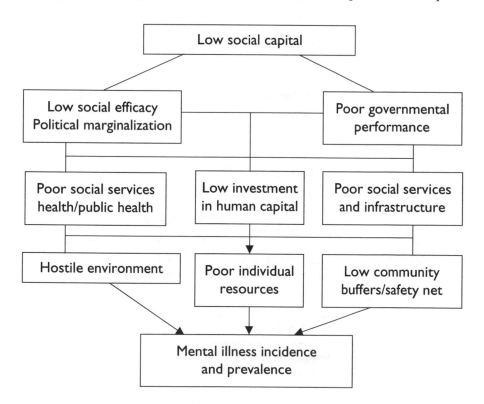

Figure 2.4 Mechanism linking vertical social capital to rates of mental illness

safety net itself, to accrue sufficient support for investment in human capital (such as a high level of education for all) and to encourage wider government to develop relevant policies that will help develop a good social infrastructure. The social environment, social safety net and educational resources in the community will be lower. This would decrease the ability of the community to help people who are getting into difficulty back towards a state of psychological balance. Hence, in such a community, rates of mental health problems could be considered likely to increase.

In Figure 2.5, there is an attempt to link the speculative models that we have discussed so far. The central spine illustrates the move from vulnerability to becoming ill or preclinical symptoms to the development of incident illness, and that illness becoming chronic or prevalent. It allows for social factors to be seen to influence the vulnerability of the population as well as the progression towards mental illness. The right-hand side of the figure illustrates the impact that social capital has on individuals and communities, while the left-hand side shows the impact of social capital on governance.

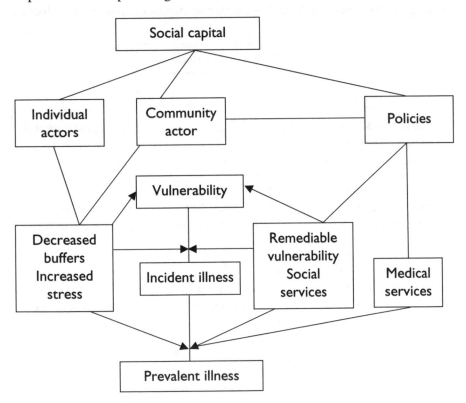

Figure 2.5 Composite mechanism linking individual, community and vertical impacts on individual pathway balance to illness

Conclusion

We are a long way short of demonstrating that social capital causes mental illness or answering our three questions:

- Can social capital prevent mental illness?
- Can lack of social capital cause mental illness?
- Does the level and type of social capital in an area have an impact on the rate of mental illness in that area?

With causal mechanisms not researched and inconclusive results from longitudinal research, it could be argued that there is a need for significant caution before considering social capital as a viable basis for preventive strategies. This may well be so, but the aim of this chapter was not to build a case for social capital to be the current basis of policy but to offer models that will help us to think about how it could be linked to mental illness and to help the reader interrogate the case studies in Part 2 of this book.

As stated previously, risk and association are not the same as causation. However, it is helpful to use the lens of causation to develop our thinking, and it will be useful to remember this context when considering how studies of the association between social capital and mental illness are set up, what the methodological problems are and what we can learn from them.

References

Cullen, M., Whiteford, H. (2001) *Interrelations of Social Capital with Mental Health.* Canberra: Commonwealth of Australia.

De Silva, M., McKenzie, K., Harpham, T., Huttly, S. (2005) Social capital and mental illness: a systematic review. *Journal of Epidemiology Community Health 59,* 619–627.

Diez-Roux, A.V. (1998) Bringing context back into epidemiology: variables and fallacies in multilevel analysis. *American Journal of Public Health 88,* 216–222.

Gelder, M., Mayou, R., Cowen, P. (2004) *Shorter Oxford Textbook of Psychiatry Part 1.* Oxford: Oxford University Press.

Kawachi, I., Berkman, L. (2000) Social cohesion, social capital, and health. In L. Berkman and I. Kawachi (eds) *Social Epidemiology.* New York: Oxford University Press.

Kawachi, I., Kennedy, B.P., Lochner, K., Prowthrow-Stith, D. (1997) Social capital, income inequality, and mortality. *American Journal of Public Health 87,* 1491–1498.

Lavis, J., Stoddart, G. (1999) Social cohesion and health. McMaster University Centre for Health Economics and Policy Analysis Working Paper Series 99–09.

McKenzie, K., Whitley, R., Weich, S. (2002) Social capital and mental illness. *British Journal of Psychiatry 181,* 280–283.

Prince, M., Harwood, R.H., Blizard, R.A., Thomas, A., Mann, A.H. (1997) Impairment, disability and handicap as risk factors for depression in old age: the Gospel Oak Project V. *Psychological Medicine 27,* 311–321.

Sampson, R., Groves, W. (1989) Community structure and crime: testing social-disorganization theory. *American Journal of Sociology 94*, 774–802.

Whitley, R., McKenzie, K. (2005) Social capital and psychiatry: review of the literature. *Harvard Review of Psychiatry 13*, 71–84.

CHAPTER 3

Systematic review of the methods used in studies of social capital and mental health

Mary De Silva

One international medical literature search engine, Medline, cites well over 150 studies examining the association between social capital and health (Kawachi *et al.* 2004) and many hundreds more exploring the relationship between social capital and non-health-related outcomes. Social capital is starting to influence mental health policy development (Cullen and Whiteford 2001; Department of Health 2001; Henderson and Whiteford 2003), despite the lack of a clear evidence base and coupled with wide-ranging criticisms of the concept. One of the most serious of these criticisms is that the measurement of social capital does not match up to the theory (Woolcock 1998; Stone 2001; McKenzie *et al.* 2002).

In order for social capital to be a useful concept, the criticisms surrounding its conceptualization and measurement must be addressed. This chapter reports the findings of a systematic review of published quantitative studies examining the association between social capital and mental health. It will evaluate the methods used by those studies in the light of existing criticisms of social capital research. It will explore how studies that measure the association between social capital and mental health have conceptualized and measured social capital. It will document the major limitations of the research to date. On the basis of this review, it will make recommendations for the methodology of future research.

Procedure

This review aimed to identify all published quantitative studies investigating the association between social capital and mental illness up to December 2004.

Seventeen electronic databases and electronic resources were searched using text word and thesaurus terms related to mental health and social capital. In addition, 'in press' articles of the two journals that publish the majority of social capital and health research (*Social Science and Medicine* and the *Journal of Epidemiology and Community Health*) were hand-searched to identify forthcoming papers. As different terms were, and still are, used to describe what has now been joined under the umbrella term 'social capital', a wide range of search terms was used, for example 'social cohesion' and 'collective efficacy'. Exploded mesh headings were used to search for all mental health outcomes. The reference sections of studies identified in this way were hand-searched to identify additional papers.

The search identified over 25,000 abstracts. Papers were included if they had a mental illness outcome, including suicide (Harris and Barraclough 1997), but excluded if they measured only subthreshold states. An example would be the inclusion of studies that measured as an outcome alcohol-dependency syndrome, which is an *International Classification of Diseases*, 10th revision (ICD-10) category with specific criteria for diagnosis, but not studies where the outcome is binge drinking or heavy alcohol use, which are not diagnostic categories.

Studies only were included if they made explicit reference to the concept of social capital, either by calling the measure 'social capital' or by explicitly grounding the measure in social capital research. A panel of experts blind to the origins of the papers reviewed the methods sections of studies to decide whether there was a mental illness outcome and whether social capital had been measured.

Methodological characteristics of the studies were reviewed (for example, study design and setting), the measure of social capital was examined and the methodological limitations of the studies were documented.

Characteristics of studies

Twenty-eight papers satisfied the inclusion criteria. Other papers either did not measure mental illness or did not measure social capital. Table 3.1 summarizes the methodological characteristics of the studies and Appendix 3.1 lists the methods and main results of each study.

Only a limited range of mental health outcomes are explored by the studies, with the majority (17/28) using screening instruments for common mental disorders (anxiety and depression).

Henderson and Whiteford's (2003) critique of the literature stated that social capital's association with common mental disorders should be explored first, as it is unlikely to be associated universally with the whole range of mental disorders. From this review, it would seem that much of the research that predates Henderson and Whiteford's comments did focus on common mental disorders.

Other mental health outcomes included childhood mental disorders, use of mental health services, psychosis, suicide and substance misuse.

Table 3.1 Description of studies*

	No. of studies
Level of measurement of social capital	
Individual	21
Ecological	8
Mental health outcome	
Adult common mental disorders	17
Child mental health	5
Mental health service use/care	5
Psychosis	1
Substance misuse	1
Suicide	1
Study type	
Cross-sectional	20
Longitudinal	8
Case–control	2
Setting	
North America	14
Europe, excluding the UK	8
UK	4
Australia	2
Developing countries	1
Site	
Mixed	15
Urban	12
Rural	1
Total no. of studies	28

* These categories total more than 28, as some studies fitted more than one category. For example, some studies used both cross-sectional and longitudinal methods or measured more than one mental health outcome.

The studies are set in a limited geographical range, with only one of the 28 studies coming from the developing world (Harpham *et al.* 2004) and half being set in North America. Urban populations are overrepresented, in particular the urban poor.

Measurement of social capital

Conceptualization of social capital

The way in which the studies defined and conceptualized social capital lends credence to the criticism that social capital as a concept is used very broadly. Studies encompassed all social relationships at any level, including within families, within communities and between state-level organizations (Macinko and Starfield 2001; Muntaner *et al.* 2001; Fine 2002; McKenzie 2003).

The majority of studies adopt the view that social capital is ecological, which is reflected in the structure of social relationships, but a number of studies use an individualistic definition as the resources that accrue to individuals as a result of their membership of social networks. A further school of thought is represented by three studies that adopt a definition of social capital as being embedded in the social relations between individuals but available as a resource to individuals. This theory was developed in relation to educational outcomes in children, and it is notable that all three papers using this definition measure child mental health (Parcel and Menaghan 1993; Furstenberg and Hughes 1995; Runyan *et al.* 1998).

None of the original theories on which measurements were based was developed in relation to health outcomes. It is unclear whether the definitions reflect those aspects of social relationships that are most important for mental health.

The principal conceptualizations define social capital as a social good, resulting in the common criticism that social capital explores only the positive side of social relations (Portes 1998; Kawachi and Berkman 2000; Macinko and Starfield 2001; McKenzie *et al.* 2002). For example, Putnam (1995) defines social capital as 'coordination and co-operation for mutual benefit' and Coleman (1990) as 'relations among actors ... that are useful for the cognitive or social development of a child or young person'. Despite this, many of the studies included in this review do acknowledge the potentially harmful effects of social capital and, in fact, measure social capital in a value-neutral way, as evidenced by the association found between group membership and worse mental health in some studies (Mitchell and La Gory 2002; Veenstra 2005).

Level of measurement

The literature can be divided into studies that consider social capital as the property of individuals and those that consider social capital as a property of groups. There is a tension between the two. The question often asked is: Which is correct?

The existing literature on social capital and mental health does little to resolve this debate, with seven studies measuring it at the ecological level, 20 at the individual level, and one at both levels (Veenstra 2005). This makes the claim that there is a 'consensus that social capital is a characteristic of social groups rather than individuals' (Shortt 2004) seem rather optimistic. The issue is complicated further by a few papers that do not state whether they measure ecological or individual social capital or indeed make any reference to the existence of the debate surrounding level of measurement. In addition, a large number of the studies using Putnam's theory, which is arguably ecological, actually measure social capital at the individual level. These studies measure either an individual's access to and participation in producing an ecological resource (i.e. the extent to which an individual is personally involved in the community through social participation) or an individual's perception of the resource (i.e. whether an individual thinks that people in general are trustworthy) rather than the resource itself.

The fact that only eight studies measure ecological social capital, three of which use the same dataset (Drukker *et al.* 2003, 2004; van der Linden *et al.* 2003), may highlight the difficulties with the measurement of ecological social capital. For instance, while six studies aggregate individual responses to the 'community level', the size of these geographical communities varies. Some measure social capital in a US state – some of these have populations and areas greater than a European country – while others measure smaller ecological units of up to 10,000 people within a European country. As in the income-inequality literature, different effects have been shown at different levels of aggregation (Wilkinson 1997). It may be that differences between the results of the ecological studies may reflect different levels of aggregation. A further difficulty is that with the exception of one study (Hendryx and Ahern 2001), all ecological studies included measures that are aggregations of individual responses. There is an acknowledged need for contextual measures that do not require aggregation of individual responses or rely on individual perceptions that may be confounded by mental health status (Henderson and Whiteford 2003; McKenzie *et al.* 2002), but in practice such measures are elusive. One example (Veenstra 2005) used per capita number of public spaces as a proxy for structural social capital. However, the use of proxy measures of context can lead to problems in itself. Do public spaces really measure social capital? Other contextual proxy measures are similarly problematic, for instance voting rates (Rosenheck *et al.* 2001; Greenberg and Rosenheck 2003; Desai *et al.* 2005), are open to different interpretations. The degree to which voting is confounded by cultural factors such as political history is unclear.

Contextual measures of ecological social capital may also be questioned on conceptual grounds. In the social-support literature, perceptions of support are as important as actual support. Is it the actual level of community social capital that is important or the community's perception of the level of social capital? If social capital has its impact on health through psychological mechanisms, then it could be argued that a community's perception of social capital is at least as important as the actual contextual measurement of social capital.

Can individual and ecological social capital be reconciled? Pollack and von dem Kneseback (2004) argue that the two are not mutually exclusive and that 'the degree to which the individual level infuses with the neighbourhood level and vica versa requires further theoretical and empirical study'. Indeed, it seems that research into the two streams is so entrenched that it would be naive to assume that either one can be ignored. However, taking a holistic view of social capital as the 'value' of social relationships at any level allows the two streams not only to coexist but also to complement each other. Individual social capital considers direct relationships with a network (i.e. the impact of an individual participating in or perceiving a network), while ecological social capital considers the indirect relationships (i.e. the impact of networks irrespective of participation). For example, effective community networks that prevent the closure of a local hospital benefit everyone who depends on that hospital, not only those people involved in campaigning against the closure. As it is not necessary to be part of the campaign group to benefit from its actions, this is an example of an indirect relationship. However, there may also be an additional impact on those involved personally in the group (direct effects), with positive effects such as feelings of self-worth and negative effects such as time and emotional investment. In order to measure the indirect effects of ecological social capital on an individual's mental health, the direct effects of that individual's own social capital must also be controlled for, i.e. the impact of the community resource *irrespective* of the individual's own resources. Statistical modelling using multilevel techniques can be used to separate out these contextual and compositional effects.

Diversity of social capital measures

The social capital measures used in the 28 papers largely confirms Wall *et al.*'s (1998) assertion that 'there is a point where diverse interpretations create more confusion than clarity. Social capital is on the threshold of being used so widely and in such divergent ways that its power as a concept is weakened'. The papers measure 11 different aspects of 'social capital', as outlined in Table 3.2. Table 3.3 lists the main methodological limitations of the studies.

Of the 11 aspects of social capital that have been measured, eight reflect common definitions of social capital. Three of these eight relate to cognitive measures of social capital (Harpham *et al.* 2002) (trust, social cohesion, sense of

Table 3.2 Measures of social capital used in studies

Social capital measure	No. of studies
Structural social capital	

Group membership

Individual   10

- Participation in voluntary or local organizations. Frequency measured occasionally.

Ecological   4

- Per capita membership of voluntary organizations. Per capita number of public spaces.

Engagement in public affairs

Individual   8

- Citizenship – involvement in local civic action, e.g. attending meetings, demonstrating, voting in elections.
- Informal social control – willingness to intervene in hypothetical neighbourhood-threatening situations, e.g. children misbehaving, opening of brothel.

Ecological   3

- Voting rates.

Social support

Individual   6

- Actual social support – extent of help received from neighbours for different needs, e.g. helping if someone is sick, support from co-workers.
- Perceptions of social support – neighbours willing to help in theoretical situations, e.g. taking care of children.
- Reciprocity.

Ecological   3

- Social contacts with neighbours.

Community networks

Individual   6

- Informal social contacts with neighbours, bridging social ties with dissimilar people, contact with friends and family.

Continued on next page

Table 3.2 cont.

Social capital measure	No. of studies

Cognitive social capital

Trust

Individual   13

- Generalized (thin) trust – would you say in general that people can be trusted?
- Trust in institutions, e.g. politicians, community leaders, government.
- Thick trust – trusting people in specific tasks.
- Security of employment contract.

Ecological   4

- Average level of generalized trust.
- Average level of trust in politicians.

Social cohesion

Individual   7

- Social harmony – getting along with neighbours, close neighbourhood, people know each other, degree to which neighbours are aware and supportive of actions, e.g. watch out for children.

Sense of community

Individual   6

- Feeling at home in neighbourhood, rating community as a place to live, neighbourhood attachment, community integration.

Other

Neighbourhood problems

Individual   4

- Perceptions of neighbourhood problems, safety and crime levels.

Family social capital

- Family structure – e.g. single-parent family, number of children.
- Family characteristics – e.g. work patterns of mother, emotional support from parents to children.

Healthcare social capital

Ecological

- Community level of healthcare insurance.
- Collaborations among healthcare organizations.

Table 3.3 Methodological limitations of studies

Methodological limitation	No. of studies
Measurement of social capital	
Includes measures that do not reflect common definitions of social capital	10
Secondary analysis of survey questions not originally designed to measure social capital	6
Does not measure all aspects of social capital (cognitive and structural)	12
Combines different aspects of social capital into one score	10
No information on validity of social capital measure	24
Measurement of mental health	
Non-validated measure of mental health	1
Methodological limitations of study which may bias results	
One community type sampled, so little variation in social capital scores between individuals	5
Potential selection bias – response rate less than 60%	9
Features of analysis that may bias results	
Hierarchical data structure, but only single-level modelling used – inappropriate analysis	2
No control for confounding by socioeconomic status	6
Variables on causal pathway included in model, e.g. neighbourhood disorder	6
Total no. of studies	28

community), four relate to structural social capital (group membership, engagement in public affairs, social support, community networks), and one relates to Coleman's definition of family social capital, which, while rooted in theory, has so little in common with the other measures that the results from these studies have to be viewed separately.

Three of the 11 measures do not fit any of the three major definitions outlined above. Hendryx and Ahern (2001) frame their work within Putnam's definition of social capital and yet measure 'community-level healthcare social capital' operationalized as collaborations among healthcare organizations and the proportion of the community with public health insurance. Liukkonen *et al.*

(2004) measure 'workplace social capital' with security of employment contract (which they call an indicator of trust) and social support from co-workers combined into a score of high or low social capital. Lastly, four studies include measures of neighbourhood disorder or safety despite these not appearing in the original definitions of the concept. This resulted in tautological arguments by measuring both the causes and the consequences of social capital (Portes 1998).

Further heterogeneity is caused by six of the studies retrofitting concepts of social capital on to existing survey questions rather than developing questions specifically to measure social capital, resulting in measures such as voting rates acting as crude proxies (Rosenheck et al. 2001; Greenberg and Rosenheck 2003; Desai et al. 2005).

The net result is that the studies purporting to measure social capital in relation to mental health are actually measuring a disparate group of exposures.

It seems that social capital has been a victim of its own success, with researchers labelling related but distinct concepts as social capital and thereby weakening the theoretical robustness of the concept. This process started with the theoretical confusion stemming from three very different conceptualizations of the term (Bourdieu 1986; Coleman 1988; Putnam 1993) and has been compounded by the adoption of these different schools of thought by researchers from different disciplines, with little or no rationalization of the disparate streams.

Adding to the confusion, some researchers have deliberately not called their measures 'social capital' despite direct overlap with the theoretical constructs of social capital. Shortt (2004) identifies a range of overlapping terms, including 'social cohesion', 'sense of community', 'collective efficacy' and 'community competence', which reflect aspects of social capital and concludes that 'undertherorization has rendered social capital susceptible to confusion with related terms'.

The broad search terms used for the systematic search ensured that papers that measured aspects of social capital but did not specifically call them social capital were identified. In addition to the 28 papers included in this review that used the term 'social capital', 11 papers were identified that measured aspects of social capital but did not identify with the concept. Because of our methodology, these papers were not entered into the review. Thus, nearly a third of 'social capital' and mental health research to date has explicitly not used the term 'social capital'.

These studies fall into two main types: those that measure social cohesion (Aneshensel and Sucoff 1996; Cutrona et al. 2000; Ross et al. 2000; Ellaway et al. 2001; Curtis et al. 2004; Silk et al. 2004; Young et al. 2004) and those that measure group membership (Wright 1990; Brown et al. 1992; Rietschlin 1998). In addition, one paper called the exposure 'sense of community' (Gatrell et al. 2004). All of these papers were published after 1990, and seven of them after 2000, and thus it may be that researchers simply chose not to identify their research with the social capital literature rather than that they were unaware of the concept. This increasing trend towards measuring single aspects of social capital, such as group membership, and not relating this to the wider social capital literature is, perhaps, a direct response to criticisms of the concept. It could be seen as an attempt by researchers to be more conservative and accurate in their reporting.

To further add to the confusion surrounding the measurement of social capital, even when researchers *claim* to be measuring the same aspects, they may actually be measuring different things. For example, 'civic participation' is used by some researchers to describe engagement in public affairs (Harpham *et al.* 2004) and by others to refer to membership of community groups (Ziersch and Baum 2004). Trust in people in general is variously called 'social trust' (Desai *et al.* 2005), 'generalized trust' (Lindstrom 2004), 'thin trust' (Harpham *et al.* 2004) and 'community trust' (Veenstra 2005).

Unidimensional measures of social capital

Many of the social capital measures used by the studies in this review do not match the complexity of recent theory, which recognises that social capital is a multidimensional concept. Only one study in the review measures bridging social capital (Mitchell and La Gory 2002), and none explicitly measures bonding or linking social capital. Instead, most studies measure aspects of cognitive and structural social capital.

The simplicity of measurement is evidenced further by 12 of the studies measuring only one aspect of social capital, such as social cohesion or group membership, rather than trying to measure different dimensions. In addition, ten of the studies that do measure more than one aspect combine the results into one score of high or low social capital. This makes it difficult to explore the interrelations between different aspects of social capital and to explore the relative importance of different aspects of social capital for health.

The validity of combining disparate measures is unclear. Those studies that have separated out different aspects of social capital have found that their effects on mental health vary (e.g. Mitchell and La Gory 2002).

The questions used to measure aspects of social capital in the studies may not capture important within-concept variation. For example, community per capita membership of organizations when used as a measure does not capture any of the complexity of type of group membership, or extent of involvement, both of which may be important.

A number of more recent studies have used complex measures, such as membership of different group types both inside and outside the community (Harpham *et al.* 2004; Ziersch and Baum 2004), and frequency of participation in the group (Pollack and von dem Kneseback 2004). Distinguishing between different group types may be important, as qualitative interviews in Australia have shown that respondents make a link between involvement and poor mental and physical health for some group types (e.g. community action groups), whereas other types of groups such as sports and social groups are seen to be beneficial to health (Ziersch and Baum 2004). However, it does depend on whether the aim is to measure group membership as an ecological or individual measure. It is unclear whether groups that are considered useful by an individual are also useful from an ecological point of view. At an ecological level, some may argue that adding the complexity of individual assessment of a group is unwarranted in the assessment of community structure. There is a danger of ecological and atomistic fallacy.

Similar patterns can be seen with the measurement of trust. While some studies have used a range of questions to capture a variety of different types of trust such as thin and thick trust, and trust in institutions (e.g. Harpham *et al.* 2004), the majority measure only generalized trust, using variations of the question 'Do you think people in general can be trusted?' However, as Blaxter (2004) argues, it is not clear that complex questions measuring many dimensions of trust are any better than simple questions, and qualitative research may be useful to compare these types of questions.

Lastly, the measurement complexity that does exist is often lost in the analysis, for example with different group types collapsed into one score of amount of group membership, or many different questions being collapsed into one score using factor analysis. Much more work is needed to tease out those dimensions of social capital that are most important for mental health, and this may require more complex measurement.

Validation of social capital tools

Van Deth's (2003) plea that 'assessing the validity of each measure of social capital in different settings (both cross-cultural and longitudinal) should be standard practice among empirical researchers in this area' has not been heeded. Only four of the 28 papers reported psychometric validation (internal reliability) of the social capital tools they used (Runyan *et al.* 1998; Caughy *et al.* 2003; Pevalin and Rose 2003; Pevalin 2004). The rest made no reference to validation. A broader search of the literature encompassing all social capital tools found only 12 studies attempting some validation, the majority being psychometric (De Silva *et al.* 2006). This is an indictment of the low level of measurement sophistication in the field in general.

However, as Bowden *et al.* argue (2002), psychometric validation does not contain any analysis from the respondents' viewpoint, a perspective that is vital in order to understand how respondents interpret the questions and, therefore, what the questions are actually measuring. Three of the 12 studies did use cognitive validation techniques (Boreham 1999; Earthy *et al.* 2000). One of the studies compared standard psychometric validation techniques with a qualitative validation using cognitive interviewing techniques for a tool to measure social capital in Peru and Vietnam (De Silva *et al.* 2006).

This analysis showed that standard validation techniques alone are not sufficient to adequately validate multifaceted social capital tools for use in different cultural setting, as they rely on data already collected by the tool and therefore are not capable of eliciting what the questions are actually measuring.

These results and those of the other qualitative studies show significant differences between what the researchers believed they were asking and the way in which the respondents interpreted the questions. For example, studies from the UK, Peru and Vietnam all showed that questions relating to generalized trust were problematic, as respondents were unable or unwilling to comment about people they did not know personally and, therefore, could not comment on people in general (Earthy *et al.* 2000; Blaxter and Poland 2002; De Silva *et al.* 2006).

Validation studies have also highlighted problems with the definition of 'community' used by studies measuring community social capital. Blaxter (2004) argues that it is very difficult to measure aspects of communities when many different communities are intermingled in urban areas with no definite boundaries, or where communities are in a state of continual change, for example because of people moving into and out of the area. The definitions of 'community' in the studies included in this review varied enormously, from US states of five to ten million people (Desai *et al.* 2005; Greenberg and Rosenheck 2003), through large metropolitan statistical areas (Hendryx and Ahern 2001), to smaller census blocks of 5000–10,000 (Caughy, O'Campo *et al.* 2003). These areas were chosen essentially for ease of measurement rather than to reflect respondents' definitions of their community; only a few studies attempted to use respondent-based definitions (e.g. Ziersch and Baum 2004; Ziersch *et al.* 2005).

The findings from two UK studies demonstrated that respondents referred to different geographical areas, depending on the question being asked (Boreham 1999; Earthy *et al.* 2000). In interviews with 31 respondents in southern England, Earthy *et al.* (2000) found that when asked about community services, respondents talked about the area within a 15-minute walk from their home. However, when asked about trust in people in general, they referred only to their street or immediate vicinity.

Interviews with 35 elderly residents in the UK found that 'community' 'was a word almost never used' by respondents (Blaxter and Poland 2002). However, in Vietnam, where 'commune' is a resilient and highly meaningful geographical construct, no such problems were encountered (De Silva *et al.* 2006). These studies highlight the need for a culturally specific geographical frame of reference to be used to define community.

While generic tools are often used to measure social capital in different cultural settings, Szreter and Woolcock (2004) argue that social capital is a product of the history of political, constitutional and ideological developments in any given setting. As such, it is important to validate any generic tool in each cultural setting in which it is to be applied. The organizations and social networks that are important for structural social capital may differ between different cultures, while culture may affect perceptions of social relationships (cognitive social capital), for example notions of trust. This means that the same question may be interpreted differently in different cultural settings, and culturally specific questions may need to be asked in order to capture the range of social capital available. Only one of the studies compared the relationship between the same measures of social capital and mental health in different countries (Pollack and von dem Kneseback 2004). This study found significant differences in the level of social capital between the USA and Germany; for example, in the USA, 81.2 per cent of respondents had participated in a church or charity situation in the past month, compared with only 30.2 per cent in Germany. However, this sort of participation may be more relevant in the USA than Germany, where other forms of community participation predominate; therefore, community participation in Germany is underestimated. It remains unclear how much this reflects different interpretations of the question versus actual differences.

Methodological limitations of studies

As listed in Tables 3.1 and 3.3, the studies to date that have examined the association between social capital and mental health are subject to a number of methodological limitations that restrict the strength of conclusions that can be drawn. Principal among these is the predominance of cross-sectional studies (22/28), which makes the direction of association between social capital and mental health impossible to determine. It is highly plausible that mental illness could result in reduced social participation and distrust, rather than the other way round. Results from the eight longitudinal studies are very promising, with all five of the studies using Putnam-style measures of social capital showing a significant protective effect of some aspects of social capital on mental health (Rosenheck *et al.* 2001; Pevalin and Rose 2003; Pevalin 2004; Sundquist *et al.* 2004; Desai *et al.* 2005). The two longitudinal studies that use Coleman-inspired measures of family social capital (Parcel and Menaghan 1993; Furstenberg and Hughes 1995) and the study measuring 'workplace social capital' (Liukkonen *et al.* 2004) show more varied results.

Five studies are also limited by a lack of diversity in their datasets, whereby data are sampled from the same community type, resulting in little variation in social capital scores and a corresponding lack of power to detect an effect on mental health. Nevertheless, most studies display analytical sophistication, with all ecological social capital studies and even some individual-level studies using appropriate multilevel modelling techniques, while the vast majority control adequately for confounding by socioeconomic status.

Results of the studies

The results of the systematic review have been reported with regard to the associations between mental illness and social capital (De Silva *et al.* 2005).

In brief, the results from these studies are varied. They provide evidence for associations between some social capital measures with some mental health outcomes. Where an association is reported, cognitive social capital (such as norms of trust and reciprocity) is associated with better mental health. Structural social capital (participation), although largely associated with better mental health, was also found to be associated with poorer mental health in some studies.

The diversity of results may be explained by the wide range of the outcomes and social capital measures examined by the studies. It suggests that the link between the two is complex and varies between settings.

Conclusion

This review highlights the limitations of research conducted to date and lends some credence to the criticism that the current measurement of social capital does not match up to the theory. Too many studies use unidimensional measures of social capital or rely on unvalidated tools or questions not originally designed to measure social capital. The problem of how to validate social capital tools remains one of the major challenges facing this research (Macinko and Starfield 2001; Harpham *et al.* 2002).

The most serious charge against social capital is the lack of theoretical rationalization resulting in little agreement as to what social capital is and, consequently, how to measure it. The debate about which level social capital should be measured does little to resolve the issue. This theoretical diversity results in related but distinct concepts being included under the umbrella term 'social capital', a situation that, if left unresolved, could lead to the consignment of social capital to the 'unproven' dustbin of academic ideas.

It is unrealistic to expect that a single definition of social capital can be adopted from the three existing schools of thought or that researchers will come to a consensus as to whether social capital is the property of groups or individuals. The least we can expect, however, is for studies to identify themselves with one of the schools of thought and to state clearly which measure of social capital they are using and at what level. Only then can we begin to evaluate systematically the strength of evidence for each type of social capital and decide which, if any, is the most important for mental health.

Despite these problems, there remains cause for optimism. The trend towards increasing measurement sophistication with more recent studies using multidimensional measures capable of exploring the impact of different aspects of social capital on mental health is promising. This increasing measurement complexity is mirrored by analytical sophistication through the use of multilevel analyses adjusted appropriately for a wide range of confounding factors. The evidence to date suggests that the relationship between social capital and mental health varies by setting, aspect of social capital, and mental health outcome. It is not a magic bullet or a cure-all pill. Only sophisticated measurement and analytical tools are capable of eliciting the true complexity of the relationship. Without them, the promise of social capital research may remain unfulfilled and the research may not offer enough information on which to base the development of interventions.

Recommendations for future research
Measurement of social capital

- State clearly which school of thought the measure relates to and the level at which social capital is being measured.
- The complexity of social capital theory should be matched by multidimensional tools. This requires appropriate development, piloting and external validation of tools for the context in which they are to be used.
- Research into the effects of bridging, bonding and linking social capital to see whether it is the nature of relationships that is important (i.e. cognitive and structural social capital) or where those relationships take place.
- More research into community-level measures of social capital is needed. So far, the promise of social capital as a community resource has not been tested adequately, as so few studies have explored community-level effects.

Methodological issues

- More longitudinal research is needed.
- There is a need for research comparing different population groups and diverse communities to ensure adequate variation in social capital in order to pick up any effects on mental health.
- There is a need for more research in low-income countries and in rural populations.
- Explicit hypotheses about mechanisms linking social capital to mental health need to be developed and tested.

Appendix 3.1 Characteristics of the 28 studies measuring social capital and mental health

Study	Setting, design, sample size	Mental health measure	Unit of analysis	Social capital measure	Limitations
Putnam: trust and social participation					
Veenstra (2005)	Canada XS 1194 adults from 25 communities	Depression (11-question scale)	Individual and community, aggregate and contextual	Individual: participation in voluntary organizations, trust in politicians, community leaders and government, and community trust measured by perceptions of helpfulness in community	5, 6, 8
				Community: per capita number of public spaces, per capita membership of voluntary organizations, average level of community and political trust	
Desai *et al.* (2005)	USA L 121,933 adults	Death from suicide after one year among patients discharged from a veterans' psychiatric inpatient programme	State, aggregate and contextual	Community organizational life (e.g. level of membership in local organizations), engagement in public affairs (e.g. voting rates), community volunteerism, informal sociability (e.g. social contacts with neighbours), and social trust (e.g. belief that other people are trustworthy)	2, 4, 5, 10
Greenberg and Rosenheck (2003)	USA XS 725 adults from 139 medical centres	Continuity of mental health care	State, aggregate and contextual	As above	2, 4, 5, 10

Continued on next page

Appendix 3.1 cont.

Study	Setting, design, sample size	Mental health measure	Unit of analysis	Social capital measure	Limitations
Rosenheck et al. (2001)	USA L 2668 adults from 18 communities	Recovery among homeless people with severe mental health; psychotic problems = C-DIS-R and PERI; alcohol and drug problems = Addiction Severity Index	Community, aggregate and contextual	As above	2, 4, 5, 10
Mitchell and La Gory (2002)	USA Urban poor XS 222 adults	CMD Modified CES-D	Individual	Bonding = participation in community Bridging = trust, bridging social ties with dissimilar people	5, 7, 11
Pollack and von dem Kneseback (2004)	USA and Germany XS 1290 aged 60+ years	CMD CES-D	Individual	Reciprocity, generalized trust, monthly participation in local organizations	5, 8
Lindstrom (2004)	Sweden XS 13,604 adults	CMD GHQ	Individual	Social participation during the past year (13 questions), generalized trust in other people; grouped into high social capital (high trust/high participation), 'miniaturisation of community' (low trust/high participation), traditionalism (high trust/low participation) and low social capital (low trust/low participation)	4, 5, 8, 10

Study	Sample	Outcome	Level	Social capital measure	Refs
Boreham et al. (2003)	England national sample XS 7988 aged 16+ years	CMD GHQ12	Individual	Perceived social support, contact with family, contact with friends, trust, participation in organized activities, neighbourhood problems, ease of access to services	1, 5, 11
Ziersch et al. (2005)	Australia Urban XS 2400 adults from one city district	CMD SF-12 mental health subscale	Individual	Neighbourhood connections, generalized trust, reciprocity, neighbourhood safety, local civic action	5, 11
Harpham et al. (2004)	Columbia Urban poor XS 1060 15–25-year-olds	CMD SRQ20	Individual	35 questions grouped into 8 factors measuring group participation, general, thick and thin trust, social cohesion, informal social control and civic participation	5, 7
Putnam: social participation					
Sundquist et al. (2004)	Sweden L 9170 24–74-year-olds	First admission to hospital due to psychiatric illness without substance abuse	Individual	Social participation score based on 17 questions relating to participation in social activities and socialization with and between neighbours	3, 4, 5

Continued on next page

Appendix 3.1 cont.

Study	Setting, design, sample size	Mental health measure	Unit of analysis	Social capital measure	Limitations
Ziersch and Baum (2004)	Australia Urban XS 530 adults from two suburbs	CMD SF-12 mental health subscale	Individual	Involvement in 10 types of civil society groups inside and outside the local area in the past 12 months	3, 5, 7, 8
Sampson: informal social control and social cohesion and trust					
Stevenson (1998)	USA Urban XS 160 African American adolescents	CMD Multi-score depression index (MDI)	Individual	11-item scale measuring the degree to which a person perceives his or her neighbours to be aware and supportive of his or her activities, i.e. 'Do your neighbours watch what you or other children in your neighbourhood do?'	1, 3, 4, 5, 7, 10, 11
van der Linden et al. (2003)	The Netherlands Urban CC 262 6–13-year-olds from 36 neighbourhoods in Maastricht	Child mental health service use	Community, aggregate	2 scales: informal social control = willingness to intervene in hypothetical neighbourhood-threatening situations, e.g. children misbehaving or opening of brothel; social cohesion and trust = bonds and trust among residents, i.e. 'People are willing to help their neighbours, this is a close-knit neighbourhood'	3, 5, 8
Drukker et al. (2004)	The Netherlands Urban CC 3411 adults from 35 neighbourhoods in Maastricht	Adult mental health service use	Community, aggregate	As above	3, 4, 5, 8

Study	Setting/Sample	Measure	Level	Description	
Drukker et al. (2003)	The Netherlands Urban XS 576 11-year-olds from 35 neighbourhoods in Maastricht	Child health questionnaire mental health and behaviour subscales	Community, aggregate	As above	3, 5, 8
Steptoe and Feldman (2001)	England Urban XS 658 adults from 38 postcode sectors	CMD GHQ_12	Individual	As above	3, 8, 11
Sense of community/neighbourhood attachment					
Caughy et al. (2003)	USA Urban XS 200 3–4.5-year-old African American children	Child behaviour checklist	Individual	13 items measuring psychological sense of community divided into two factors: general sense of community (i.e. sharing values with neighbours, getting along and feeling at home in neighbourhood) and knowing neighbours	3, 9
Greiner et al. (2004)	USA XS 4254	CMD Single question on depression	Individual	Community rating ('How would you rate your community as a place to live?') and civic participation in past 5 years (action to address community problem)	4, 5, 8, 10

Continued on next page

Appendix 3.1 cont.

Study	Setting, design, sample size	Mental health measure	Unit of analysis	Social capital measure	Limitations
Saluja *et al.* (2003)	USA XS 215 6-year-olds	Child behaviour checklist	Individual	30 questions collapsed into three factors: neighbourhood trust, neighbours' relationships with children, and extent of help received from neighbours	3, 5
Pevalin (2004)	UK national sample XS L 2328 aged 16+ years co-habiting married couples	CMD GHQ12	Individual	Eight questions on neighbourhood attachment collapsed into one score and dichotomized into lowest quartile versus rest	2, 3
Pevalin and Rose (2003)	UK national sample XS aged 16+ years Social participation = 16,750 Neighbourhood attachment = 7974	CMD GHQ12	Individual	Social participation, level of contact with friends, extent of crime in neighbourhood, neighbourhood attachment (as above)	1, 2, 11

	L aged 16+ years Social participation = onset = 35,907 person-years Recovery = 8840 person-years Neighbourhood attachment = onset = 5840 person-years Recovery = 1429 person-years	Onset, recovery from, and time to recovery from CMD measured using GHQ12	Individual	As above	1, 2, 5
O'Brien et al. (1996)	Russia Rural XS 482 adults from 3 villages	CMD Modified CES-D	Individual	Number of people in helping networks (e.g. number who help with a variety of household needs for example trading goods and services, helping if someone is sick) Community integration – how well respondent feels they 'fit' into the community	1, 3, 5, 9

Coleman: family characteristics

Runyan et al. (1998)	USA XS 667 2–5-year-olds	Child development = BDST Child behaviour = CBCL combined into 'child doing well: yes/no'	Individual	Two parent figures in home, social support of mother, no more than two children in home, neighbourhood support, and regular church attendance grouped into one index	1, 4

Continued on next page

Appendix 3.1 cont.

Study	Setting, design, sample size	Mental health measure	Unit of analysis	Social capital measure	Limitations
Parcel and Menaghan (1993)	USA L 524 6–8-year-olds	Change in child behaviour problems	Individual	Family working characteristics (i.e. number of hours, occupational complexity), family characteristics (i.e. number of children, divorce, home environment)	1, 5
Furstenberg and Hughes (1995)	USA Urban poor L 252 adolescents	CMD depression scale	Individual	Parents' social investment in their children (e.g. emotional support from mother, father in home, frequency of seeing siblings or grandparents), families' links to community (e.g. religious involvement, help network, neighbourhood as a place for children to grow up)	1, 2, 3, 5, 7
Other measures					
Hendryx and Ahern (2001)	USA Urban XS 43,278 adults and children from 43 metropolitan statistical areas	Adult and child mental health service use	Metropolitan statistical areas, contextual	Community-level healthcare social capital – collaborations among healthcare organizations and community level of public health insurance	1, 5
Liukkonen et al. (2004)	Finland L 6028 employees	CMD GHQ12	Individual	Workplace social capital – security of employment contract and social support from co-workers combined into score of high/low social capital	1, 4, 5

Key: BDST, Battelle Developmental Inventory Screening Test; CBCL, Child Behaviour Checklist; CC, case–control; C-DIS-R, Computerised Diagnostic Interview Schedule (Revised); CES-D, Centre for Epidemiological Studies–Depression Scale; CMD, common mental disorders; GHQ12, General Health Questionnaire 12; L, longitudinal; PERI, Psychiatric Epidemiology Research Interview; SF-12, Short form 12 Health Survey; SRQ20, Self Reporting Questionnaire 20; XS, cross-sectional.

Methodological limitations:

Measurement of social capital

1, Definition of social capital does not match standard definitions/includes measures that do not reflect cognitive or structural dimensions of social capital; 2, Secondary analysis of survey questions not originally designed to measure social capital; 3, Does not measure all aspects of social capital (cognitive and structural); 4, Combined different aspects of social capital (i.e. structural and cognitive) into one score rather than analysing the component parts separately; 5, No information on validity of social capital measure.

Measurement of mental health

6, Non-validated measure of mental health.

Methodological limitations of study that may bias results

7, Sampled from one community type, so little variation in social capital scores between individuals; 8, Potential selection bias – response rate less than 60%.

Features of analysis that may bias results

9, Hierarchical data structure (individual- and community-level variables), but only single-level modelling used – inappropriate analysis; 10, No control for confounding by socioeconomic status; 11, Neighbourhood disorder, violence or psychological resources adjusted for. These variables may be on the causal pathway between social capital and mental health, thus making the relationship non-significant.

References

Aneshensel, C.S., Sucoff, C.A. (1996) The neighborhood context of adolescent mental health. *Journal of Health and Social Behaviour 37*, 293–310.

Blaxter, M. (2004) Questions and their meanings in social capital surveys. In A. Morgan and C. Swann (eds) *Social Capital for Health: Issues of Definition, Measurement and Links to Health.* London: Health Development Agency.

Blaxter, M., Poland, F. (2002) Moving beyond the survey in exploring social capital. In C. Swann and A. Morgan (eds) *Social Capital for Health: Insights from Qualitative Research.* London: Health Development Agency.

Boreham, R. (1999) *Social Capital and Health: Cognitive Pilot Report.* Personal communication.

Boreham, R.M., Stafford, M., Taylor, R. (2003) *Health Survey for England 2000: Social Capital and Health.* London: The Stationery Office.

Bourdieu, P. (1986) The forms of social capital. In J. Richardson (ed) *The Handbook of Theory and Research for the Sociology of Education.* New York: Greenwood Press.

Bowden, A., Fox-Rushby, J.A., Nyandieka, L., Wanjau, J. (2002) Methods for pre-testing and piloting survey questions: illustrations from the KENQOL survey of health-related quality of life. *Health Policy and Planning 17*, 322–330.

Brown, D.R., Gary, L.E., Greene, A.D., Milburn, N.G. (1992) Patterns of social affiliation as predictors of depressive symptoms among urban blacks. *Journal of Health and Social Behaviour 33*, 242–253.

Caughy, M.O., O'Campo, P.J., Muntaner, C. (2003) When being alone might be better: neighborhood poverty, social capital, and child mental health. *Social Science and Medicine 57*, 227–37.

Coleman, J.S. (1988) Social capital in the creation of human capital. *American Journal of Sociology 94*, 95–120.

Coleman, J.S. (1990) *Foundations of Social Theory.* Cambridge, MA: Harvard University Press.

Cullen, M., Whiteford, H. (2001) *Interrelations of Social Capital with Mental Health.* Canberra: Commonwealth of Australia.

Curtis, L., Dooley, M.D., Phipps, S.A. (2004) Child well-being and neighbourhood quality: evidence from the Canadian National Longitudinal Survey of Children and Youth. *Social Science and Medicine 58*, 1917–1927.

Cutrona, C.E., Russell, D.W., Hessling, R.M., Brown, P.A., Murry, V. (2000) Direct and moderating effects of community context on the psychological well-being of African American women. *Journal of Personality and Social Psychology 79*, 1088–1101.

Department of Health (2001) *Making it Happen: A Guide to Mental Health Promotion.* London: The Stationery Office.

Desai, R.A., Dausey, D.J., Rosenheck, R.A. (2005) Mental health service delivery and suicide risk: the role of individual and facility factors. *American Journal of Psychiatry 162*, 311–318.

De Silva, M.J., Harpham, T., Tran, T., Bartoleni, R., Penny, M.E., Huttly, S.R. (2006) Psychometric and cognitive validation of a social capital measurement tool in Peru and Vietnam. *Social Science and Medicine 62*, 941–953.

De Silva, M.J., McKenzie, K., Huttly, S.R., Harpham, T. (2005) Social capital and mental illness: a systematic review. *Journal of Epidemiology and Community Health 59*, 8, 619–627.

Drukker, M., Kaplan, C., Feron, F., van Os, J. (2003) Children's health-related quality of life, neighbourhood socio-economic deprivation and social capital: a contextual analysis. *Social Science and Medicine 57*, 825–841.

Drukker, M., Driessen, G., Krabbendam, L., van Os, J. (2004) The wider social environment and mental health service use. *Acta Psychiatrica Scandinavica 110*, 119–129.

Earthy, S., Maltby, S., Arber, S.L., Cooper, H. (2000) The use of cognitive interviewing to develop questions on social capital for the 2000/1 General Household Survey. *Survey Methodology Bulletin 46*, 24–31.

Ellaway, A., MacIntyre, S., Kearnes, A. (2001) Perceptions of place and health in socially contrasting neighbourhoods. *Urban Studies 38*, 2299–2316.

Fine, B. (2002) They f**k you up those social capitalists. *Antipode 34*, 796–799.

Furstenberg, F.F., Hughes, M.E. (1995) Social capital and sucessful development among at risk youth. *Journal of Marriage and the Family 57*, 580–592.

Gatrell, A.C., Popay, J., Thomas, C. (2004) Mapping the determinants of health inequalities in social space: can Bourdieu help us? *Health and Place 10*, 245–257.

Greenberg, G.A., Rosenheck, R.A. (2003) Managerial and environmental factors in the continuity of mental health care across institutions. *Psychiatric Services 54*, 529–534.

Greiner, K.A., Li, C., Kawachi, I., Hunt, D.C., Ahluwalia, J.S. (2004) The relationships of social participation and community ratings to health and health behaviors in areas with high and low population density. *Social Science and Medicine 59*, 2303–2312.

Harpham, T., Grant, E., Thomas, E. (2002) Measuring social capital within health surveys: key issues. *Health Policy and Planning 17*, 106–111.

Harpham, T., Grant, E., Rodriguez, C. (2004) Mental health and social capital in Cali, Colombia. *Social Science and Medicine 58*, 2267–2277.

Harris, E.C., Barraclough, B. (1997) Suicide as an outcome for mental disorders. *British Journal of Psychiatry 170*, 205–228.

Henderson, S., Whiteford, H. (2003) Social capital and mental health. *Lancet 362*, 505–506.

Hendryx, M.S., Ahern, M.M. (2001) Access to mental health services and health sector social capital. *Administration and Policy in Mental Health 28*, 205–218.

Kawachi, I., Berkman, L. (2000) Social cohesion, social capital, and health. In L. Berkman and I. Kawachi (eds) *Social Epidemiology*. Oxford: Oxford University Press.

Kawachi, I., Kim, D., Coutts, A., Subramanian, S.V. (2004) Commentary: reconciling the three accounts of social capital. *International Journal of Epidemiology 33*, 700–704.

Lindstrom, M. (2004) Social capital, the miniaturisation of community and self-reported global and psychological health. *Social Science and Medicine 59*, 595–607.

Liukkonen, V., Virtanen, P., Kivimaki, M., Pentti, J., Vantera, J. (2004) Social capital in working life and the health of employees. *Social Science and Medicine 59*, 2447–2458.

Macinko, J., Starfield, B. (2001) The utility of social capital in research on health determinants. *Milbank Quarterly 79*, 387–427.

McKenzie, K. (2003) Concepts of social capital: author's reply. *British Journal of Psychiatry 182*, 458.

McKenzie, K., Whitley, R., Weich, S. (2002) Social capital and mental health. *British Journal of Psychiatry 181*, 280–283.

Mitchell, C., La Gory, M. (2002) Social capital and mental distress in an impoverished community. *City and Community 1*, 199–222.

Muntaner, C., Lynch, J., Smith, G.D. (2001) Social capital, disorganized communities, and the third way: understanding the retreat from structural inequalities in epidemiology and public health. *International Journal of Health Services 31*, 213–237.

O'Brien, D., Patsiorkovski, V., Dershem, I., Lylova, O. (1996) Household production and symptoms of stress in post-Soviet Russian villages. *Rural Sociology 61*, 674–698.

Parcel, T.L., Menaghan, E.G. (1993) Family social capital and children's behaviour problems. *Social Psychology Quarterly 56*, 120–135.

Pevalin, D.J. (2004) Intra-household differences in neighbourhood attachment and their associations with health. In C. Swann and A. Morgan (eds) *Social Capital for Health: Issues of Definition, Measurement and Links to Health.* London: Health Development Agency.

Pevalin, D., Rose, D. (2003) *Social Capital for Health: Investigating the Links Between Social Capital and Health Using the British Household Panel Survey.* London: Health Development Agency.

Pollack, C., von dem Kneseback, O. (2004) Social capital and health among the aged: comparisons between the United States and Germany. *Health and Place 10*, 383–391.

Portes, A. (1998) Social capital: its origins and applications in modern sociology. *Annual Review of Sociology 24*, 1–24.

Putnam, R. (1993) *Making Democracy Work: Civic Traditions in Modern Italy.* Princeton, NJ: Princeton University Press.

Putnam, R. (1995) Bowling alone: America's declining social capital. *Journal of Democracy 6*, 65–78.

Rietschlin, J. (1998) Voluntary association membership and psychological distress. *Journal of Health and Social Behavior 39*, 348–355.

Rosenheck, R., Morrissey, J., Lam, J., *et al.* (2001) Service delivery and community: social capital, service systems integration, and outcomes among homeless persons with severe mental illness. *Health Services Research 36*, 691–710.

Ross, C.E., Reynolds, R., Geis, K. (2000) The contingent meaning of neighbourhood stability for residents psychological well-being. *American Sociological Review 65*, 581–597.

Runyan, D.K., Hunter, W.M., Socolar, R.R., *et al.* (1998) Children who prosper in unfavorable environments: the relationship to social capital. *Pediatrics 101*, 12–18.

Saluja, G., Kotch, J., Lee, L.C. (2003) Effects of child abuse and neglect: does social capital really matter? *Archives of Pediatric and Adolescent Medicine 157*, 681–686.

Shortt, S.E.D. (2004) Making sense of social capital, health and policy. *Health and Place 70*, 11–22.

Silk, J.S., Sessa, F.M., Morris, A., Steinberg, L., Avenevoli, S. (2004) Neighborhood cohesion as a buffer against hostile maternal parenting. *Journal of Family Psychology 18*, 135–146.

Steptoe, A., Feldman, P.J. (2001) Neighborhood problems as sources of chronic stress: development of a measure of neighborhood problems, and associations with socioeconomic status and health. *Annals of Behavioral Medicine 23*, 177–185.

Stevenson, H.C. (1998) Raising safe villages: cultural-ecological factors that influence the emotional adjustment of adolescents. *Journal of Black Psychology 24*, 44–59.

Stone, W. (2001) *Measuring Social Capital: Towards a Theoretically Informed Measurement Framework for Researching Social Capital in Family and Community Life.* Melbourne: Australian Institute of Family Studies.

Sundquist, K., Johansson, L.M., Johansson, S.E., Sundquist, J. (2004) Social environment and psychiatric illness. *Social Psychiatry and Psychiatric Epidemiology 39*, 39–44.

Szreter, S., Woolcock, M. (2004) Health by association? Social capital, social theory, and the political economy of public health. *International Journal of Epidemiology 33*, 1–18.

van der Linden, J., Drukker, M., Gunther, N., Feron, F., van Os, J. (2003) Children's mental health service use, neighbourhood socio-economic deprivation, and social capital. *Social Psychiatry and Psychiatric Epidemiology 38*, 507–514.

van Deth, J.W. (2003) Measuring social capital: orthodoxies and continuing controversies. *International Journal of Social Research Methodology 6*, 79–92.

Veenstra, G. (2005) Location, location, location: contextual and compositional health effects of social capital in British Columbia, Canada. *Social Science and Medicine 60*, 2059–71.

Wall, E., Ferrazzi, G., Schryer, F. (1998) Getting the goods on social capital. *Rural Sociology 63*, 2, 300–322.

Wilkinson, R.G. (1997) Comment: income inequality and social cohesion. *American Journal of Public Health 87*, 1504–1506.

Woolcock, M. (1998) Social capital and economic development: toward a theoretical synthesis and policy framework. *Theory and Society 27*, 151–208.

Wright, L.K. (1990) Mental health in older spouses: the dynamic interplay of resources, depression, quality of the marital relationship, and social participation. *Issues in Mental Health Nursing 11*, 49–70.

Young, A.F., Russell, A., Powers, J.R. (2004) The sense of belonging to a neighbourhood: can it be measured and is it related to health and well being on older women? *Social Science and Medicine 59*, 2627–2637.

Ziersch, A., Baum, F. (2004) Involvement in civil society groups: is it good for your health? *Journal of Epidemiology and Community Health 58*, 493–500.

Ziersch, A.M., Baum, F.E., Macdougall, C., Putland, C. (2005) Neighbourhood life and social capital: the implications for health. *Social Science and Medicine 60*, 71–86.

PART 2

International studies

CHAPTER 4

Ethnographic investigation of social capital and mental health in Gospel Oak, London, UK

Rob Whitley

Gospel Oak is a small neighbourhood in north-west London that has been under epidemiological scrutiny since the early 1980s. Known together as 'the Gospel Oak Project', epidemiological surveys were conducted at regular intervals, principally with elderly residents of the neighbourhood, in an attempt to explore the link between individual-level factors such as social support and mental health outcomes. They confirmed previous research and speculation that individual-level factors such as lack of social support and loneliness tend to be associated with poorer mental health (Livingstone *et al.* 1990; Prince *et al.* 1997, 1998). Interestingly, these studies also found that prevalence of common mental disorder (CMD) among elderly people hovered around 17 per cent throughout the timespan of the Gospel Oak Project. This was significantly higher than that found in other comparable cities in the British Isles, such as Dublin and Liverpool (Copeland *et al.* 1999).

Perhaps the most significant papers arising from the Gospel Oak Project were published in the late 1990s, especially those emphasizing the role of individual-level social factors in the aetiology and maintenance of mental distress. It should also be noted that the late 1990s also witnessed a political watershed in the UK and a consequent change of tone regarding the relationship between health and society. In 1997, a centre-left Labour government took power for the first time since 1979, with a different orientation towards health and health policy. Whereas the previous Conservative government had talked about 'health variations', the new Labour government talked of 'health inequalities'. The new government's White Paper *Our Healthier Nation* (Department of Health 1998) stated explicitly that the root causes of ill-health must be tackled as a priority to improve public health. Social and environmental factors in the aetiology of illness are emphasized throughout the White Paper. The White Paper also made mental health one of the government's four key target areas for improvement. Indeed, British Prime Minister Tony Blair stated in October 1999: 'Depression is a particular concern, which costs lives, and affects the quality of life. We can achieve goals ... but only if we tackle the underlying social, economic and environmental conditions as well as the specific causes' (Dawson and Tylee 2001).

At about the same time as research interest in Gospel Oak was intensifying and the new British government was issuing declarations about the important impact of social conditions on mental health, interest was growing in the concept of social capital among academics and policy-makers throughout the world. The World Bank has embraced the concept, issuing various discussion papers and even developing an Internet forum devoted to the subject (www.worldbank.org/poverty/scapital/htm). Winter (2000) also notes how journal articles using social capital as an identifier increased nine-fold when comparing the period 1991–1995 with the period 1996–1999.

It is thus entirely understandable that in this political and academic climate, researchers working on the Gospel Oak Project should begin to look beyond the hitherto closely examined individual-level risk factors to the possible effect of neighbourhood context on mental health. In doing so, social capital presented itself as a very appropriate heuristic that could be applied to assist investigation.

Social capital, mental health and Gospel Oak
As stated previously, prevalence of CMD among elderly people in Gospel Oak appears to be higher than that found in similar anglophone cities. Although the epidemiological surveys were useful in establishing the existence of these reported health inequalities, they were limited in what they could say about why mental distress may be elevated in this specific neighbourhood. The surveys did find that loneliness and social-support deficits appeared to be linked significantly to mental distress in the elderly samples under study. However, the question remained open as to whether a third supra-individual-level factor could help to explain both the overall high rate of CMD and some of the prevalent individual-level social CMD risk factors. Speculation began over whether this third factor could be social capital or, more accurately, lack of social capital in the neighbourhood.

This was an intriguing theoretical possibility, supported to some extent by wider existing literature. The Roseto study in Pennsylvania, USA, suggested that communities with stronger social ties suffered less heart disease (Wolf and Bruhn

1993). Similarly, the Alameda county study in California reported that excess mortality may be related to social context (Haan *et al.* 1987). To investigate the question of how far rates of CMD in Gospel Oak were related to social capital (or lack thereof) required some form of systematic 'social diagnosis' of the Gospel Oak neighbourhood. Ongoing quantitative research could contribute to this community portrait, but it was thought that qualitative research, hitherto unemployed in the Gospel Oak Project, could provide complementary depth and understanding to the relationship between social capital and mental health in Gospel Oak. Thus, in 1999, the Gospel Oak Project added a qualitative researcher to investigate the link between social capital and mental health in Gospel Oak, and the Gospel Oak Project expanded from an epidemiological study *in* a defined neighbourhood to an ethnographic study *of* a defined neighbourhood.

Investigating social context

Studies of social capital vary in both their conceptual orientation and their chosen methodological approach. I have written elsewhere about how social capital is sometimes modelled as a property of individuals and sometimes as a property of place/groups (Whitley and McKenzie 2005). Conceptualizing social capital as a property of place may be a theoretical advance on pre-existing literature, as it goes beyond conventional social support/network theory. However, this conceptualization of social capital as shared social context is notoriously difficult to operationalize, investigate and measure (Frohlich *et al.* 2002). Although collecting data from individuals can give indications about social context, this methodology runs the risk of numerous biases, most notably the 'atomistic fallacy', the fallacious extrapolation of individual data to the group level. Investigation of social context is also hampered by the fact that there is no consensually accepted or validated screening instrument that can be used to measure social capital or social context. Previous studies have used proxy variables of varying utility, ranging from simple binary questions asking people about their trust of others (e.g. Subramanian *et al.* 2001) to studies relying on in-depth interviews (e.g. Cattell 2001).

In an attempt to overcome some of these challenges, I decided to utilize a mix of qualitative methods in an attempt to make a 'social diagnosis' of shared social context in Gospel Oak and its impact on residents' mental health. First, in-depth interviews were used in order to access individual residents' perceptions and impressions of social and neighbourhood life in Gospel Oak. Twenty-six interviews were conducted in total. Second, focus groups were used to discover whether randomly selected groups of individual residents would reach consensus on social context in Gospel Oak and, if so, what this consensus may be; two such groups were conducted. Third, I collected and analysed documents produced within and about Gospel Oak in order to discern how these documents constructed Gospel Oak as a lived environment. Finally, I engaged in long-term (two years) participant observation. This latter method was vitally important, as it introduced an element of independent assessment into the methodological equation. As participant observer, I would regularly spend large amounts of time in the neighbourhood. The participant observation was conducted in a variety of milieus. This included documenting level and uptake of public/private services in the neighbourhood, attending community meetings and churches, talking to key informants such as shopkeepers and spending time in public spaces in order to observe interactions and everyday social life. The overall aim was to build a 'thick description' of life in Gospel Oak that could be used to explore the hypothesis that the rate of CMD observed in the neighbourhood could be somewhat explained by a relative lack of social capital.

Whitley and Prince (2005a) found that in interviews, residents generally expressed satisfaction with trust and community facilities in the area and engaged in a number of confirmatory behaviours, for example looking after neighbours' keys or borrowing on credit. Elsewhere, I have described the difference in tone between documents produced by third parties about Gospel Oak (generally negative) when compared with views of residents (generally positive) as expressed in interviews and focus groups (Whitley and Prince 2005b). In this chapter, I will focus on how data gathered through participant observation contributed to the 'social diagnosis' of the neighbourhood, which could help elucidate the research question concerning social capital and mental health. In this research, the orientation of Putnam (1993, 2000) regarding conceptualization of social capital is taken, whereby social capital is seen to consist primarily of trust, horizontal networks and neighbourhood involvement – quite close to what non-social scientists term simply 'community spirit'.

Services and facilities

One of the first things I did and then repeated at regular intervals as a participant observer was to conduct what I labelled a 'neighbourhood audit'. This involved walking around Gospel Oak once a week, for between half a day and a whole day, noting the provision and utilization of services and facilities in the neighbourhood. I tried to vary my days/hours of walking throughout the two-year period in order to ensure my observation captured any temporal variation. During observation, I would list all the services and facilities in the neighbourhood and make qualitative field notes regarding usage, as well as note my own personal impressions regarding ambience in these services and facilities. I would then return to my office, where I would group together services and facilities according to type and make some analysis regarding the extent to which they may be indicative of social capital in the neighbourhood. Table 4.1 describes some of the services and facilities observed and their principal characteristics. This is in no way an exhaustive list of facilities and services in Gospel Oak but simply represents those with which I became in some way acquainted during the course of the research. They also appeared, in retrospective analysis, to play a prominent role in the formation and continuation of social capital in Gospel Oak.

The mere existence of these diverse facilities within a small neighbourhood suggested to me that social capital may be well-developed in Gospel Oak. Jacobs (1961) called the existence of prominent local facilities 'landmarks' that bring residents together, allowing horizontal networks and mutual trust to flourish. This line of thought regarding the role of shared social facilities goes back as far as William Cobbett (1985), whose seminal work *Rural Rides* famously lamented the enclosure of open commons in nineteenth-century England as being instrumental in breaking the bonds that tied together rural dwellers. In the absence of common land from which people gathered food or took their animals to graze, places were limited in which trust and social ties could develop between people living in the same locality.

It would be erroneous to infer that social capital is rich in Gospel Oak from a mere enumeration and description of key facilities. Ethnographic assessment relies on investigating the meaning and impact of these facilities on everyday life. Thus, I spent varying amounts of time in all of the services and facilities listed in Table 4.1 in order to understand how far they were contributing to the build-up of social capital in Gospel Oak. Data generated were enormous, and so in the interests of brevity I will describe two selective examples of field work conducted in the services/facilities. As I have previously described Queen's Crescent Library and Queen's Crescent Community Centre (Whitley and Prince 2005a) I will focus the remainder of this section on Kentish Town City Farm and local religious organizations. These have been selected because they are representative of the wider dataset and should be considered as giving indications of social capital/community spirit in Gospel Oak.

Kentish Town City Farm

Kentish Town City Farm is spread over five acres lying close to the heart of the Gospel Oak neighbourhood. It is open 9.30 a.m. to 5.30 p.m. Tuesday to Sunday; entrance is free. The farm houses a variety of animals, including horses, poultry, sheep and goats. Horse-riding lessons are given to children, and I often witnessed people of all ages tending the sheep and goats. There are also plots for local pensioners to grow food. I estimated there were between 30 and 50 plots. Many of the plots appeared very productive, and I saw, among other fruits and vegetables, a rich harvest of tomatoes, onions, potatoes and various herbs.

Table 4.1 Services and facilities in Gospel Oak encountered during participant observation

Services/facilities	Brief description
Council-funded community resources	
Queen's Crescent Community Centre	Principal local community centre running diverse groups and events
Queen's Crescent Library	Local library consisting of main library, children's library and computer/training suite
Kentish Town City Farm	City farm with various animals and vegetable plots utilized by all age groups
Talacre Square and Sports Fields	Open space, sports field
Gospel Oak Astroturf Field	Floodlit astroturf field used for football and basketball
Religious organizations	
Gospel Oak Methodist Church	
St Martin's Church of England	
St Dominic's Roman Catholic Priory	
Health services and facilities	
Royal Free Hospital	Large University of London teaching hospital on edge of neighbourhood
Gospel Oak Health Clinic	Local health clinic
Retail outlets	
Queen's Crescent shops and market	Long street of shops with over 50 different outlets, including cafés, take-aways, pubs, pharmacist, GP's surgery, petshop, bookmaker, and baker
	Site of twice-weekly street market

Services/facilities	Brief description
Lismore Circus shops	Collection of around ten outlets in the north of Gospel Oak
Public transport	
Gospel Oak railway station	Station on north London line
Hampstead Heath railway station	As above
Chalk Farm underground station	Underground station on Northern Line
Kentish Town underground station	As above
Belsize Park underground station	As above
Various bus routes	
Other prominent services/facilities	
Hampstead Heath	Large popular open space immediately to the north of Gospel Oak
Lido swimming pool	Heated open-air swimming pool
Hampstead Heath sports facilities	Sports centre for athletics
Gospel Oak district housing office	Housing office run by the local authority

At the entrance to the farm was an education centre that offered classes to children and adults. The farm produces a quarterly newsletter called 'Farm News', which is created by schoolchildren who work on the farm, the editor being 15 years old in the summer of 2000. The farm also produces Kentish Town City Farm T-shirts and a recipe book. In its own mission statement, the farm states: 'The farm allows local people to get involved in activities such as animal care, horse riding, gardening. It also provides opportunities for schools, youth work and community events' (Kentish Town City Farm 2000).

I conducted participant observation at the farm on a weekly basis. I always found it busy, lively and friendly. On an average day, most of the people there were schoolchildren, who came either with a school group or after school. I observed many parents with their young children in attendance at weekends. The local authority (Camden Council) organized activities at the farm in the summer, such as the Camden Summer Playscheme. The formal work carried out by the staff was mostly with young people. The mostly elderly people who worked the vegetable plots at the back of the farm tended to get on with their own activities. In fact, I found an atmosphere of intergenerational cohesion at the farm, as younger and older people were often working together on common goals, for example collecting blackberries from bushes at the back of the farm. In addition to the paid staff were a number of (many local) volunteers, including offenders on probation. It is possible for local people to receive training to non-vocational qualification level in aspects of farm management. Below is an extract from my field notes taken during a visit to the farm in August 2001:

> It was a warm and sunny summer afternoon as I approached the farm. I went inside the door of the City Farm and was greeted with a sign asking me to disinfect my shoes because of recent concerns over foot and mouth disease. This action I gladly took. I noticed straight away the sound and sight of many young children; ages probably between 8–15, who all seemed intensely occupied in some activities. They were either doing something with the horses, goats and sheep or were following the adults who seemed to be teaching something. There were only a few adults about at the entrance to the farm, one had a T-shirt on saying 'Camden Summer Playscheme'. A number of poultry crossed my path as I slowly walked down the main pathway of the farm. As I reached the back end of the farm I saw a number of elderly people tending their vegetable plots. Some were talking to each other while others were singing to themselves. I greeted them and they greeted me back. I engaged in some small talk regarding their likely harvest and they all seemed quite optimistic, though they were worried foot and mouth might lead to closure of the farm altogether. At the very back of the farm is a horse enclosure surrounded by blackberry bushes. I started picking some blackberries and eating them by the railway track. This point of the farm is slightly elevated compared with the rest and I thus had a good vantage-point to observe the farm's activities. After a while, a woman leading a horse came my way with two children following; she put the horse in a pen. The kids tried to get some blackberries but they were out of reach. They politely asked me if I would get some for them. I said yes and obliged. They then started talking to the elderly people and laughing and joking...

My overall independent assessment of the farm and its role in the Gospel Oak community was positive. It appeared to fulfil the classic 'landmark' functions alluded to by Jacobs and the 'commons' function alluded to by Cobbett. It provided a communal space where residents could meet one another and engage in positive action. It brought together dissimilar people (i.e. older and younger people) and thus extended networks and built trust among neighbours, fulfilling Putnam's criteria for the development of social capital.

Religious organizations

Durkheim (1951) stated the importance of religious activity and how it is symbolic of wider community in an area. During participant observation in the religious organizations, I thus attempted to measure not only the relationship between religious organizations and their members but also, perhaps more importantly, what they did for the wider community. This latter point may be more important in measuring social capital and is thus prioritized in this section.

My participant observation with regards to religious organizations was limited to three local churches representing mainstream Christianity (Anglican, Methodist, Roman Catholic). I was conscious that there were at least two other churches in Gospel Oak of a Pentecostal/Evangelical orientation. I was also aware of a mosque on Queen's Crescent, which always looked very busy on a Friday early evening. However, I restricted my activities to the three mainstream churches, partly because initial field work suggested that these were the most prominent neighbourhood religious organizations.

A cursory glance at any of the three local newspapers revealed that all three churches organized regular non-religious events that were open to and utilized by local residents of all faiths (including no faith). The Roman Catholic Priory had monthly concerts, held on a Friday or Saturday, usually in the form of an organ recital or string quartet. The Anglican church held similar music events. It also organized other successful and well-attended cultural events, such as the staging of the play 'Thomas à Becket' in November 2000, involving professional and amateur local actors and ancillary crew. The Anglican minister was praised by non-religious people I encountered during participant observation as being active in the wider community, for example printing and distributing a leaflet to local households offering comfort and counselling after a local suicide. The Methodist church also held regular non-religious events, such as jumble sales and a monthly Good Soup Café, open for anyone to have a cheap hearty lunch. I attended many of these events and found that they were usually fairly well-attended and welcoming to outsiders (like me). I noticed that two sections of society disproportionately attended or supported these religious activities as well as more conventional religious activities such as Sunday services; these were elderly people and people from ethnic minority communities. In fact, specific churches seemed to be hubs of local ethnic minority activity; for example, a large proportion of the congregation at the Roman Catholic Priory was Hispanic or Irish, whereas at the Methodist church there were more African and Caribbean members.

Taken in the round, my assessment of the activity conducted by these three organizations overlapped very well with data I collected at Kentish Town City Farm, at Queen's Crescent Library and at Queen's Crescent Community Centre. All of the data were suggestive of an alive, involved and horizontally connected neighbourhood community.

Community groups and meetings

Lochner *et al.* (1999) stated that collective efficacy and psychological sense of community were two key components of social capital. I thus attempted to tap into these two concepts by collecting data during participant observation on lobbying groups, voluntary organizations and regular local events. Again, the aim was to provide a 'thick description' from which appropriate inferences could be made. Table 4.2 describes events and meetings that I attended during the course of the research. It is by no means exhaustive, and organizations/groups/events have been chosen for their prominence, as assessed by myself at the end of the research.

Again, the mere existence and levels of participation may be suggestive of extensive neighbourhood social capital. Many of the groups were devoted to suggesting or trying to achieve change in Gospel Oak. Although most of these groups and events had a convivial ambience, others, for example the District Management Committee and the Gospel Oak Partnership Board, were often characterized by conflict and sometimes heated argument, usually over issues such as neighbourhood management, perceived broken promises and allocation of resources. This conflict and argument frequently played itself out in the letters page of local newspapers, and some key informants raised it with me as a problem in the local community. My own independent assessment tended to agree with the key informants who suggested that there was an element of division amongst community leaders as well as some officials, but this did not appear to suggest that the Gospel Oak community was overly dysfunctional. In light of the rest of the data, these divisions appeared minor; many ordinary residents were not even aware of the conflict existing at a higher level. Similarly, rather than indicating a pathological community, the fact that some local people felt passionate and confident enough to form lobbying groups such as Gospel Oak Community Concern that could voice relevant concerns may indicate a positively vibrant neighbourhood community.

The divisions in the community are mentioned mainly to indicate the complexity of social relations in Gospel Oak, which is being necessarily simplified in this short chapter. I am not suggesting that the neighbourhood is without problems, and I discuss these, most notably fear of crime, in more detail elsewhere (Whitley and Prince 2005c). I am simply emphasizing that associational involvement, horizontal networks and trust did not appear to be overly problematic in Gospel Oak from my point of view of participant observer. This point can be illuminated through an extract from my field diary describing one of the events listed in Table 4.2 – the Gospel Oak Working Parties Joint Meeting held in January 2001. This was a one-off event at which key relevant officials and local residents reported back on the debates and advances made in ongoing working groups over the past year (examples of working groups include the health working group and the elderly working group).

Table 4.2 Public events and meetings in Gospel Oak attended during participant observation

Group/event	Regularity	Attendance	Notes
Gospel Oak Partnership Board	Monthly	20–50	Liaison group between community and council regarding regeneration
Gospel Oak Partnership Board: Health Working Party	Monthly	10–20	Group discussing health matters in Gospel Oak
Gospel Oak Partnership Board: Elderly Working Group	Quarterly	About 10	Group discussing elderly matters in Gospel Oak
Gospel Oak District Management Committee	Quarterly	About 50	Committee of local authority officials and community representatives discussing housing issues
Gospel Oak Community Forum	Irregular	10–20	Community group discussing local issues
Camden Central Community and Police Consultation Group	Quarterly	20–30	Liaison group between police and community discussing crime
Senior Citizens' Luncheon Club	Daily	20–30	Lunch club in Queen's Crescent Community Centre
Gospel Oak Spring Health Fair	One-off	60+	Health fair held in April 2000
Gospel Oak Community Safety Meeting	One-off	30+	One-off meeting on community safety
Queen's Crescent Summer Festival	Annually	200+	Day-long festival held annually in July
Gospel Oak Working Parties Joint Meeting	One-off	50+	Joint meeting of working groups held in January 2001
Church services and events	Weekly	Variable	Services and events such as jumble sales and music concerts

The meeting, taking place at the Queen's Crescent Community Centre, was advertised in the local newspapers for people to come and 'find out what is happening and get involved'. Letters were also sent to people on the Gospel Oak Partnership Board mailing list. I received a letter of invitation. The event was also advertised in 'Challenge News', a free publication delivered to houses in the challenge area and available elsewhere. Lunch was provided as an incentive. The timetable was split between plenaries and workshops on the working party topics. On arrival at 11 a.m. participants were greeted by the Community Centre manager, who asked people to fill out a registration form. She sat at a table by the entrance. She gave participants a programme that also had a few others sheets attached. One of these was the weekly Community Centre schedule, which is growing by the month. I note that new clubs have recently started, such as Weight-Watchers, Somali classes and hairdressing. I picked up lots of other leaflets in the course of the day. One was an application form for Gospel Oak Gardening Club. Another was for a seniors' keep-fit class that occurred Monday and Tuesday mornings. Another one was for a new dinner club; this will be held at the Community Centre with diners buying, cooking and preparing the food themselves. Groundwork Camden (local environment charity) gave out a lot of leaflets: two were about a Gospel Oak Environmental Audit Questionnaire asking people about environmental issues affecting them that they would like to discuss further. Another leaflet was given out by the Roundhouse (local arts centre) about its developing role as a creative centre for young people (the meeting was also attended by a Roundhouse rep). About 55 people were in attendance. I counted 16 men and 35 women. Approximately four were under 30. Otherwise there was a pretty even age spread. Three were from visible minorities. The majority of the participants were paid employees from organizations. These included Camden Council, schools, GPs, etc. There was a high level of cognitive recognition though there were some newcomers who had not been seen before …

To close this section describing my social diagnosis of Gospel Oak, I quote from what is perhaps one of the finest observational accounts of rural England written in the twentieth century – Flora Thompson's *Lark Rise to Candleford*:

Fordlow might boast of its Church, its school, its annual concert, and its quarterly penny reading, but the hamlet did not envy it these amenities, for it had its own social centre, warmer, more human, and altogether preferable, in the taproom of the 'Wagon and Horses'.

(Thompson 1979, by permission of Oxford University Press)

The Wagon and Horses was of course the hamlet pub, and though there is not space to go into detail, Gospel Oak seemed to be particularly rich in 'informal' social life, such as bingo evenings, greasy-spoon cafés, pub life and sports clubs, such as boxing, darts, etc. This was written about frequently in the local newspapers and confirmed by my own participant observation. In all, the data did not suggest that residents were living in an impoverished social environment, and thus 'lack of social capital' appears to be an inadequate explanation for the high rates of CMD seen in Gospel Oak.

Strengths and weaknesses of the research

An in-depth ethnographic case study of a single urban neighbourhood has a number of strengths and weaknesses that should be discussed before drawing conclusions. One main strength of the study is that the researcher can become completely immersed in the lived day-to-day experience of the neighbourhood. Time and energy are devoted exclusively to collecting and analysing data in the one neighbourhood, providing what is often called a 'thick description'. Thus, internal validity of the results of these kinds of case study is often deemed to be high.

However, there are also weaknesses to this approach, which should be considered in the interpretation of the results of this study. First, no comparisons are being made between social capital/community spirit in other areas. I am unable to say with scientific certainty whether the levels, types and impacts of social capital in Gospel Oak are higher or lower than those seen elsewhere. Still, the speculation surrounding the causal role of social capital in the high rates of mental illness in Gospel Oak rested implicitly on the assumption that there would be a paucity of trust, networks and associational activity in Gospel Oak, and this did not appear to be the case.

Another weakness often associated with ethnographic studies is that of observer bias. Because instruments are not standardized, the researcher becomes the prime research instrument. Thus, it is possible that the researcher's own prejudices affect both strategies of data collection and selective interpretation of data. Fortunately, strategies have been developed to overcome this risk of bias, including close supervision by more experienced colleagues and collecting data by more than one method (e.g. participant observation and interviews) in order to judge overlap and discrepancy. Both of these strategies, and others, were employed in this study. I thus have confidence that the findings are an adequate representation of social capital in Gospel Oak.

Conclusion

The ethnographic component of this study married well with the results from in-depth interview and focus groups. They all converged to suggest that there was a dense, well-developed network of services, facilities, community groups and events in Gospel Oak. This appeared to build trust and community spirit in the neighbourhood. Thus, lack of social capital seemed to be an inadequate explanation of the high rates of CMD indicated by previous epidemiological surveys in Gospel Oak.

This raises a number of pertinent issues. The data could be interpreted as suggesting that individual-level factors may be more important in explaining the high rates of CMD in Gospel Oak and that neighbourhood social capital does not confer protection against CMD. However, it should be remembered that the orientation taken to social capital in this study derived from the work of Robert Putnam; this definition emphasizes horizontal linkages between individuals as well as associational activity. Other definitions conceptualize social capital as primarily embodying individual or group variations in power, resources and vertical integration (e.g. Bourdieu 1986). It may be that these kinds of inequalities, difficult to measure through an ethnographic case study, have a greater impact on mental health than the 'community spirit' orientation of Putnam.

Another possible interpretation of the results is that prevalence of CMD would be even higher in the absence of the level and type of social capital we have described, i.e. social capital could be preventing even higher rates of CMD. It is impossible to speculate on whether this is the case, but comparative ethnographic research may help answer this question.

As described earlier, researchers involved in the Gospel Oak project, including myself, seized on the academic and political zeitgeist of the time by embracing the vogue concept of social capital as a useful heuristic to investigate the possible causes behind the high rates of CMD in Gospel Oak. Although the concept of social capital did give an appropriate theoretical anchor to the study, it did not seem to be a significant factor in accounting for overall rates of CMD in Gospel Oak. The key finding of this study is simply that CMD can be highly prevalent in the presence of rich neighbourhood trust and social activity. Individual-level factors, or group-level factors beyond those documented by Putnam, may be more important in accounting for elevated communal rates of mental illness.

References

Bourdieu, P. (1986) *Forms of Capital.* New York: Free Press.

Cattell, V. (2001) Poor people, poor places, and poor health: the mediating role of social networks and social capital. *Social Science and Medicine 52*, 1501–1516.

Cobbett, W. (1985) *Rural Rides.* London: Penguin.

Copeland, J.R.M., Beekman, A.T.F., Dewey, M.E. *et al.* (1999) Depression in Europe. *British Journal of Psychiatry 174*, 312–321.

Dawson, A., Tylee, A. (2001) *Depression: Social and Economic Timebomb.* London: WHO/BMJ Books.

Department of Health (1998) *Our Healthier Nation.* London: HMSO.

Durkheim, E. (1951) *Suicide.* New York: Free Press.

Frohlich, K.L., Potvin, L., Chabot, P., Corin, E. (2002) A theoretical and empirical analysis of context: neighbourhoods, smoking and youth. *Social Science and Medicine 54,* 1401–1417.

Haan, M., Kaplan, G.A., Camacho, T. (1987) Poverty and health: prospective evidence from the Alameda county study. *American Journal of Epidemiology 125,* 989–998.

Jacobs, J. (1961) *The Death and Life of Great American Cities.* London: Penguin.

Kentish Town City Farm (2000) *Newsletter.* London: Kentish Town City Farm.

Livingstone, G., Hawkins, A., Graham, N., Blizard, B., Mann, A. (1990) The Gospel Oak Study: prevalence rates of dementia, depression and activity limitation among elderly residents in inner London. *Psychological Medicine 20,* 137–146.

Lochner, K., Kawachi, I., Kennedy, B.P. (1999) Social capital: a guide to its measurement. *Health and Place 5,* 259–270.

Prince, M., Harwood, R.H., Blizard, R.A., Thomas, A., Mann, A.H. (1997) Social support deficits, loneliness and life events as risk factors for depression in old age. The Gospel Oak Project VI. *Psychological Medicine 27,* 323–332.

Prince, M.J., Harwood, R.H., Thomas, A., Mann, A.H. (1998) A prospective population based cohort study of the effects of disablement and social milieu on the onset and maintenance of late-life depression: the Gospel Oak project VII. *Psychological Medicine 28,* 337–350.

Putnam, R. (1993) *Making Democracy Work: Civic Traditions in Modern Italy.* Princeton, NJ: Princeton University Press.

Putnam, R. (2000) *Bowling Alone: The Collapse and Revival of American Community.* New York: Simon and Schuster.

Subramanian, S.V., Kawachi, I., Kennedy, B.P. (2001) Does the state you live in make a difference? Multilevel analysis of self-rated health in the US. *Social Science and Medicine 53,* 9–19.

Thompson, F. (1979) *Lark Rise to Candleford.* Oxford: Oxford University Press.

Whitley, R., McKenzie, K. (2005) Social capital and psychiatry – Review of the literature. *Harvard Review of Psychiatry 13,* 71–84.

Whitley, R., Prince, M. (2005a) Is there a link between rates of common mental disorder and deficits in social capital in Gospel Oak, London? Results from a qualitative study. *Health and Place 11,* 237–48.

Whitley, R., Prince, M. (2005b) Are inner-cities bad for your health? Comparisons of residents' and third-parties' perceptions of the urban neighbourhood of Gospel Oak, London. *Sociology of Health and Illness 27,* 44–67.

Whitley, R., Prince, M. (2005c) Fear of crime, mobility and mental health in inner-city London, UK. *Social Science and Medicine 61,* 1678–1688.

Winter, I. (2000) *Social Capital and Social Policy in Australia.* Melbourne: Australian Institute of Family Studies.

Wolf, S., Bruhn, J.G. (1993) *The Power of Clan.* New Brunswick, NJ: Transaction Publishers.

CHAPTER 5

Social capital and quality of life and mental health in Maastricht, the Netherlands

The neighbourhood matters

Marjan Drukker, Charles Kaplan and Jim van Os

In the late 1990s, the Maastricht University Psychiatric Department reported a number of analyses of the impact of neighbourhood on mental illness (Driessen *et al.* 1998a). Social capital was recognized as a potentially important issue, although specific data were not available (Kalff *et al.* 2001). Around that time, the Dutch government and the local authorities started to consider the neighbourhood as a possible unit for policy interventions. However, evidence to support intervention at this level was limited. A municipal inquiry suggested a need for local longitudinal research (Albeda *et al.* 2001). Subsequently, civil servants from the Maastricht local authorities contacted several Maastricht university groups. A research programme including both quantitative and qualitative research was developed in meetings between the university researchers and the local authorities. Data collections started in 2000.

Our department was responsible for quantitative research on differences between Maastricht neighbourhoods in socioeconomic indicators and social capital, and their differential impact on individuals. The Maastricht Quality of Life Study (MQoL) was designed for this purpose. Outcomes of the MQoL were subjective psychological health measures in the general population and data on levels of treated psychiatric morbidity derived from the Maastricht Psychiatric Case Register.

Before presenting the results, brief working definitions of the main concepts and an outline of the methodology of the MQoL will be presented.

Neighbourhood

The investigations focused on neighbourhood-level context. Processes at the neighbourhood level are different from processes at further aggregated geographical levels, such as state or country level. For example, in the income-inequality literature, different effects have been reported at different levels of aggregation (Wilkinson 1997). We may expect analogous differences for other area measures.

The MQoL studied neighbourhoods as defined by local authorities. Boundaries follow main roads and, therefore, are ecologically meaningful (CBS 1996). These neighbourhood definitions are used widely, and Statistics Netherlands (CBS) supplies data on a variety of neighbourhood characteristics (CBS 2003). The 36 Maastricht residential neighbourhoods each have between 300 and 8500 residents (mean 3337).

Socioeconomic deprivation

Neighbourhood socioeconomic deprivation reflects the quality of neighbourhood and structural environments. Neighbourhood socioeconomic deprivation is synonymous with neighbourhood socioeconomic disadvantage, neighbourhood poverty and low neighbourhood socioeconomic status. This measure is usually composed of objective indicators, such as the proportion of unemployed people, the proportion receiving welfare and mean income.

Neighbourhood socioeconomic deprivation has been reported to affect individuals' health over and above individual socioeconomic status, thus having deleterious effects for all inhabitants regardless of whether they are poor or affluent (Sloggett and Joshi 1994; Dalgard and Tambs 1997; Leventhal et al. 2000; Diez-Roux et al. 2001).

Social capital

Previous studies have demonstrated that 'social capital' is associated with the health of both adults (Kawachi et al. 1999a; McCulloch 2001) and children (Aneshensel and Sucoff 1996).

Kawachi et al. (1997) have summarized the work of Putnam and Coleman and have 'defined' social capital as 'those features of social organisations – such as networks of secondary associations, high levels of interpersonal trust and norms of mutual aid and reciprocity – which act as resources for individuals and facilitate collective action' (Bourdieu 1986; Coleman 1990; Kawachi *et al.* 1997; Kawachi *et al.* 1999a; Putnam 1993).

Social organizations can be of different sizes, there is no agreed definition. The Maastricht research considered social capital to be a group characteristic, we focused on neighbourhood-level social capital. We applied Kawachi's conceptualization of social capital to the neighbourhood level and produced the following working definition: 'The availability of social resources, social support and social control that neighbourhood residents can count on.'

In contrast to objective socioeconomic measures at the neighbourhood level, we considered this concept to be best measured by interviewing community members, since they are the best informants about their neighbourhood.

Quality of life

The term 'quality of life' was first used after the First World War (Ormel *et al.* 1997) and has been used widely since (Nussbaum 1993). It has been defined and conceptualized in many different ways (De Vries *et al.* 1998; Landgraf *et al.* 1996; WHO 1998). General quality of life includes domains such as income, freedom and social support, while health-related quality of life is restricted to health outcomes (Katschnig *et al.* 1997).

Health-related quality of life as a subjective measure of mental state is, to a large degree, contingent on the level of psychiatric symptomatology (Berlim *et al.* 2003; Orley *et al.* 1998; Schaar and Ojehagen 2003). Therefore, quality-of-life studies in the general population shed light on the part of mental health that drives variation in quality of life.

In the present study, perceived health, perceived mental health, a vitality scale and a mental health scale (SF36 quality-of-life questionnaire (Ware and Gandek 1998)), overall satisfaction and the WHO Quality of Life-BREF (WHOQOL-BREF) (WHO 1998) have been defined as measures of health-related quality of life in adults. In addition, general health, mental health, self-esteem and behaviour scales of the Child Health Questionnaire (CHQ) (Landgraf *et al.* 1996; Wulffraat *et al.* 2001) were included as measures of health-related quality of life in children and adolescents.

Objectives and methods of the MQoL

The MQoL studied associations between neighbourhood social capital and other neighbourhood measures, such as socioeconomic deprivation and quality of life and treated psychiatric morbidity.

The University Psychiatric Department and the municipal paediatric community health services collaborated in the MQoL study, which was a longitudinal study of adolescents and their families in all Maastricht neighbourhoods (hereafter known as family cohort study). The study aimed to follow up a cohort of young adolescents aged approximately 11 years at baseline into adulthood. In addition, both parents were asked to fill in a questionnaire at baseline. Both quality of life and individual-level demographic and socioeconomic variables were included in the children's and parents' questionnaires. The neighbourhood measure of socioeconomic deprivation was based on factor analysis results of neighbourhood data obtained from the local authorities and Statistics Netherlands (CBS).

The methods of the MQoL were adapted from the Project on Human Development in Chicago Neighbourhoods (PHDCN) (Sampson et al. 1997). The neighbourhood variables and confounding factors that were studied were similar in both studies, but the main outcomes were different. The main outcomes of the PHDCN were juvenile delinquency and violence, while the MQoL focused on quality of life.

Because perceptions of social capital are always biased by individual quality-of-life status, it is difficult to disentangle cause and effect when asking about social capital and quality of life in the same group of respondents. Therefore, in order to avoid contamination by individual perceptions of the study population, social capital measures should be collected in a sample of informants independent of the study sample (Buka et al. 2003). For this reason, the MQoL similar to the PHDCN included a community survey separate from the family cohort study. The MQoL randomly selected approximately 200 inhabitants aged between 20 and 65 years from each of 36 Maastricht residential neighbourhoods using the municipal database. These inhabitants were asked to fill in and send back a questionnaire. Social capital was measured using two collective efficacy scales – the informal social control (ISC) scale and the social cohesion and trust (SC&T) scale – developed by Sampson and colleagues (Sampson et al. 1997; Sampson 1997). Both scales were translated into Dutch and back-translated into English. In order to adapt the ISC scale to the Dutch situation, five items corresponding to typical Dutch concerns were added (Drukker et al. 2003a). The ISC scale measures the willingness to intervene in hypothetical neighbourhood-threatening situations, for example in the case of children misbehaving or the opening of a brothel in the street. This scale is conceived in such a way that respondents are independent informants about their neighbours' willingness to intervene. The SC&T scale measures bonds and trust among neighbourhood residents. Both scales were aggregated to serve as neighbourhood-level measures when analysing the family cohort data. In addition, individual-level perceptions of social capital were studied. Community survey respondents were also asked about various dimensions of quality of life and individual-level demographic and socioeconomic questions.

Results

The Maastricht research can be divided into four parts:

1   Associations between the two neighbourhood social capital variables, neighbourhood socioeconomic deprivation and residential instability.

Associations between these neighbourhood factors and:

2   adults' quality of life;

3   adolescents' quality of life;

4   mental health service consumption.

Results for part 1: associations between neighbourhood factors

The main independent variables were dimensions of neighbourhood-level social capital (informal social control, social cohesion and trust). Before studying associations between social capital and various outcome measures, associations between the social capital variables and neighbourhood socioeconomic deprivation and residential instability were studied (Drukker et al. 2003a). More socioeconomically deprived neighbourhoods generally had lower levels of informal social control and lower levels of social cohesion and trust. Unfortunately, associations were so strong that collinearity problems could arise when analysing socioeconomic deprivation and social capital in the same regression model. Therefore, results of the cohort study were based on models entering the neighbourhood variables separately. Both variables and the interaction term were entered jointly only when studying interaction effects between two neighbourhood variables. Residential instability was not associated with any of the social capital measures (Drukker et al. 2003a).

The current research found evidence that lower levels of socioeconomic deprivation were associated with higher levels of social capital (Drukker et al. 2003a), but previous research has reported that close ties and mutual aid are predominant features of poor areas, enabling people to cope with poverty (Bruhn and Wolf 1979; McCulloch 2003). In addition, anecdotal evidence suggests that Maastricht social workers traditionally notice more social interactions in poor neighbourhoods than in affluent neighbourhoods. However, the results indicated that, despite these interactions, residents of poor Maastricht neighbourhoods had a lesser degree of trust in their neighbours. It is possible that residents of affluent neighbourhoods are more sensitive and, therefore, more easily annoyed with deviant behaviour of children, resulting in higher levels of informal social control. This interpretation is supported by Chicago research that reported that neighbourhoods with concentrated disadvantage were associated with sharply lower expectations for shared child control (Sampson *et al.* 1999). In addition, residents of affluent neighbourhoods may know that they can count on their neighbours when necessary. This may lead to perceptions of higher levels of social cohesion and trust.

The strong associations between neighbourhood factors support the social disorganization theory, which poses that socioeconomic deprivation and lower levels of social capital are linked (Kawachi *et al.* 1999b; Markowitz *et al.* 2001). However, only two dimensions of social capital were included; other dimensions of social capital may not be associated with socioeconomic deprivation so strongly.

Results for part 2: neighbourhood factors and adults' quality of life

The Maastricht research on adults' quality of life started with a study of the association between neighbourhood socioeconomic deprivation and adults' quality of life and the role of individual perceptions of social capital (among others) in this association. Second, neighbourhood social capital was studied. Finally, analyses were performed to place the concept of social capital in a wider perspective: social capital was hypothesized to play a role in the mechanisms of effects of neighbourhood residential instability and income inequality.

MEDIATING EFFECTS

Data from the Maastricht community survey showed evidence that neighbourhood socioeconomic deprivation was associated with lower levels of perceived health and mental health, and (albeit statistically inconclusive by conventional alpha) with lower levels of vitality (adjusted analyses) (Drukker and van Os 2003). In addition, the influence of the following three sets of individual-level mediators on the association was assessed:

- lifestyle
- housing characteristics
- perception of housing and the neighbourhood social and physical environment.

When including the set of neighbourhood perception variables in the models, associations between socioeconomic deprivation and all outcome variables disappeared. The two perception variables with the strongest mediating effects (when included one at a time) were perceptions of neighbourhood cosiness[1] and social contacts. Certain conditions, such as neighbourhood maintenance and quality of housing, will be, by definition, worse and be perceived as worse in poor neighbourhoods compared to affluent neighbourhoods, but not cosiness and social contacts. The latter are measures of social interaction rather than measures of poverty and, therefore, represent a different construct.

Although measured at the individual level, both cosiness and social contacts are related strongly to the concept of neighbourhood social capital. As these individual-level perceptions appeared to play an important role, studying neighbourhood-level social capital was a logical next step.

SOCIAL CAPITAL AND ADULTS' QUALITY OF LIFE

The parents' questionnaire of the family cohort study included a quality-of-life questionnaire, the WHOQOL-BREF (De Vries and van Heck 1995; WHO 1998). The WHOQOL-BREF questionnaire contains 25 questions measuring five domains: overall quality of life and general health; physical health; psychological health; social relationships; and the environmental domain of quality of life. Respondents answered the questions on five-point Likert scales; higher scores indicated higher levels of quality of life.

The baseline data of the family cohort study showed that both informal social control and social cohesion and trust were associated with the environmental domain of quality of life (Drukker et al. 2003b). This association remained after controlling for family socioeconomic status and other individual-level variables. In addition, social cohesion and trust were associated with physical health, but after controlling for confounders, this association was statistically imprecise by conventional statistics (Drukker et al. 2003b). There were no associations with the other domains of quality of life.

RESIDENTIAL INSTABILITY

Although residential instability was not associated with our measures of social capital (Drukker et al. 2003a), theoretically these two concepts are linked (Sampson 1997). Maintenance of social capital is difficult when the neighbours keep moving. Residents are then forced to exert effort in rekindling social contacts with new neighbours. One would expect residential instability to predict lower levels of social capital.

---

1   There is no English equivalent of the Dutch word '*gezelligheid*' that is used in
         the questionnaire. We chose the word 'cosiness', but '*gezelligheid*' is also a
         combination of closeness, warmth and friendliness.

A US study of residential instability reported interaction effects. The association between socioeconomic deprivation and wellbeing was greater in stable neighbourhoods (Ross et al. 2000).

We performed analyses to replicate these findings. Results suggested that the effects of socioeconomic deprivation were most salient in neighbourhoods with low residential turnover (Drukker et al. 2005a). Thus, in our study, residential *instability* may be beneficial in deprived neighbourhoods. The social isolation perspective invoked by Ross et al. (2000) may apply to Maastricht as well. According to this perspective, stability in poor neighbourhoods is perceived by residents as tantamount to being trapped and powerless in a dangerous and frightening place. Because of this, residential instability offers hope.

From a policy perspective, promoting residential instability of residents living in poor neighbourhoods is unlikely to be a satisfactory solution. Improving the access of residents in (stable) poor neighbourhoods to jobs and other opportunities that do not require them to move could help to overcome the feeling of being trapped.

Because of the theoretical link with social capital, living in a stable neighbourhood was expected to be beneficial both in poor and affluent neighbourhoods. Because residential stability can be seen as a dimension of social capital, higher levels of quality of life would have been expected in stable neighbourhoods. No such effect was apparent and, on the contrary, residential stability seemed to be a disadvantage in poor neighbourhoods. However, this same interaction effect also indicates that residents of affluent neighbourhoods only benefit from living in an affluent neighbourhood if this neighbourhood is stable.

INCOME INEQUALITY

Social capital has been described as one of the mechanisms explaining why higher levels of income inequality are associated with lower levels of health (Kawachi et al. 1999a). Because of this, we investigated income inequality using data from the parents of the family cohort study.

It has been argued that it may not be the absolute levels of socioeconomic deprivation, as described above, that contribute to health problems (the absolute income hypothesis), but rather that the causal factor is income inequality within a geographical unit, suggesting that everyone, poor or rich, would benefit from a more equal income distribution (the relative income hypothesis) (Kawachi et al. 1999a).

In the present study, neighbourhood-level measures of income inequality were not associated with any of the quality-of-life outcomes (Drukker et al. 2004a). These findings were in agreement with other studies using similarly small geographical or population units. In contrast, most studies at state or country level have reported associations between income inequality and health outcomes. Results of a study investigating perceived health and income inequality at different levels of aggregation demonstrated associations with income inequality at county level but not at census-tract level (Soobader and LeClere 1999). Therefore, guided by the work of Wilkinson (1997), it could be argued that the relative income hypothesis is applicable only to geographical areas with large population sizes (i.e. large counties or larger e.g. states in the US). Although most income inequality research has studied mortality, this more specific hypothesis may also be valid for quality of life (Drukker *et al.* 2004a) and perceived health (Soobader and LeClere 1999).

One of the pathways that has been proposed to underlie the relative income hypothesis is that inhabitants living in areas with higher levels of income inequality may belong to different social groups, creating social divisions that may be difficult to overcome. The resulting lower levels of social capital (e.g. vertical bridging social capital) have been associated with poor health (Kawachi *et al.* 1999a). However, this proposed mechanism involves neighbourhood-level social capital when, as discussed above, income inequality may play a role only at larger levels of aggregation. Because of this, we think that neighbourhood-level social capital may not be part of the pathway through which income inequality and health outcomes are linked.

Results of part 3: neighbourhood factors and adolescents' quality of life

ADOLESCENTS' HEALTH-RELATED QUALITY OF LIFE

Our first paper on adolescents reported associations between neighbourhood variables and adolescents' quality of life (Drukker *et al.* 2003a). At baseline, the children of the family cohort study (aged approximately 11 years) received a questionnaire including all items of the CHQ (Landgraf *et al.* 1996; Raat *et al.* 2002; Wulffraat *et al.* 2001). Our results suggested that both socioeconomic deprivation and social capital were associated with quality of life. In addition, one aspect of social capital, informal social control, was associated specifically with adolescents' mental health and behaviour. This effect is, to a large degree, independent of adolescents' general health. This specific result may be explained by compliance with norms and values. Increased social control may help adolescents to understand better which norms and values they should obey and what happens if they do not. This may impact directly on behaviour and indirectly on feelings of mental health.

DIFFERENT CULTURAL SETTINGS

The ISC and SC&T scales were adapted from the PHDCN (see Objectives and methods of the MQoL) (Sampson *et al.* 1997), which allowed comparison between that study and ours (Drukker *et al.* 2005b). For these analyses, we used the original items only (literally translated in the Maastricht questionnaires). Results indicated that Maastricht had lower levels of informal social control, while Chicago had lower levels of social cohesion and trust. In addition, informal social control showed more variation in Chicago neighbourhoods, which suggests sharper contrasts between neighbourhoods. These differences may reflect true differences in community functioning in Maastricht and Chicago or may reflect differences in the way respondents understood and answered the questions in each study.

Both the PHDCN and the MQoL included one question on perceived health, 'How do you perceive your health?', answered on a Likert scale. Associations between neighbourhood variables and this outcome variable could be analysed in both cities (Drukker *et al.* 2005b). Ethnic interaction effects were found in the data, which necessitated the PHDCN study population to be broken down into 'Hispanic-American' and 'non-Hispanic' adolescents.

The results showed that higher levels of socioeconomic deprivation and lower levels of social capital were associated with poorer perceived health in Maastricht adolescents and Chicago Hispanic adolescents. However, these associations were not found in the Chicago non-Hispanic population.

Two differences between Chicago and Maastricht may account for differences in associations. First, differences in individual incomes and, consequently, differences in neighbourhood socioeconomic deprivation are much smaller in Maastricht than in Chicago (Schama 1988). The difference in variability of income and deprivation can cause problems with comparative statistical analysis and makes results difficult to interpret. However, if this were the reason for different effects we would have expected greater effects in Chicago children than in Maastricht children. Second, the impact of government on housing may be different between the Netherlands and the USA. As a result, Maastricht neighbourhoods may be more mixed than Chicago neighbourhoods (Kleinhans *et al.* 2001), and this may explain the greater variation in informal social control in Chicago. However, variation in social cohesion and trust was similar.

In sum, associations between social capital and perceived health seem to have different magnitudes in different populations. More research is needed to investigate the populations in which social capital plays an important role, and why social capital is not associated with health outcomes in other populations.

CHILDREN'S GROWTH AND SCHOOL ACHIEVEMENT

In our study, we also measured growth and school achievement. We did not find evidence for an association between children's growth and social capital (Drukker *et al.* 2003c). We concluded that neighbourhood measures may play a role, but effects seem to be expressed more readily in the psychological rather than the physical domain in children living in Maastricht.

It has been hypothesized that adolescents from poor neighbourhoods are more often absent from school because of higher sickness rates and this may affect school performance. On initial analysis, school achievement was poorer in socioeconomically deprived neighbourhoods and in neighbourhoods with lower levels of informal social control and social cohesion and trust (Drukker *et al.* submitted a). However, after controlling for individual-level demographic and socioeconomic factors, most associations disappeared. One aspect of the neighbourhood environment, informal social control, was associated with better school achievement, but only in boys. Informal social control may play a role not only in mental health and behaviour (Drukker *et al.* 2003a) but also in school achievement of boys (Drukker *et al.* submitted a).

CHANGES IN SELF-REPORTED QUALITY OF LIFE AND BEHAVIOUR BETWEEN THE AGES OF 11 YEARS AND 13–14 YEARS

Two to three years after the baseline measurement, adolescents of the family cohort were reassessed (Drukker *et al.* submitted b). The aim was to investigate associations between neighbourhood variables and changes in quality of life. We did not find an association between neighbourhood variables and general health and mental health. While quality of life of 11-year-olds was associated with neighbourhood context in our study, quality of life of 13- to 14-year-olds was not.

There were, however, associations between neighbourhood socioeconomic deprivation and self-esteem, satisfaction and behaviour in subgroups (interaction). Adolescents had higher levels of self-esteem and satisfaction when family socioeconomic status and neighbourhood socioeconomic deprivation concurred (Drukker *et al.* submitted b). Higher levels of self-esteem in adolescents from lower-educated families in poor neighbourhoods may reflect a tendency for this group to associate with and support each other. Adolescents may be more likely to join a specific form of youth peer group (generally termed a 'gang'), which has compensatory functions for deficits in the neighbourhood and at home (Hill *et al.* 1999; Spergel 1992; Valdez 2003). Although similar groups do not exist in a small European city like Maastricht, current results suggest that psychological outcome and socioeconomic conditions are similar in Maastricht (Drukker *et al.* submitted b).

In the group of adolescents where family socioeconomic status did not concur with neighbourhood socioeconomic deprivation, there was an association between self-esteem and deprivation. The higher the deprivation, the lower the self-esteem (Drukker *et al.* submitted b). However, strong social cohesion and trust decreased this association. In addition, the follow-up data showed that socioeconomic deprivation was associated with the development of (self-reported) behavioural problems in the subgroup of children of higher-educated parents living in residential unstable neighbourhoods (unpublished results, 2005).

If we were able to demonstrate associations between social capital and quality of life using both baseline and follow-up surveys, then this would have been strong evidence for causal effects of social capital. However, not finding these associations does not rule out causality. The two to three years between baseline and follow-up may be too short to measure an effect, or the effects of social capital may be induced at earlier or later ages.

Results of part 4: neighbourhood factors and mental health service consumption

A different way to assess the contribution of social capital to mental health is to measure service use. This yields different information from quality-of-life assessment.

Data on service consumption in Maastritch have been reported previously, but only a limited set of individual confounders were included (Driessen et al. 1998a, 1998b; van Os et al. 2000). In addition, most of the studies have not differentiated between psychiatric disorders (Croudace et al. 2000; Driessen et al. 1998a).

Social capital and other contextual factors may not be associated with the full range of mental disorders; therefore, it is essential to differentiate between psychiatric disorders (Henderson and Whiteford 2003). We studied the risk of being diagnosed with a mental illness and, separately, the risk of being diagnosed with schizophrenia. We also assessed the quantity of service consumption for each group.

RISK OF SERVICE CONSUMPTION IN ADULTS

Two case–control datasets were constructed. The first one included all incident cases in the year 2000 (aged 20–65 years) registered in the Psychiatric Case Register (PCR) serving Maastricht and surroundings; community survey respondents functioned as the population control group (Drukker et al. 2004b). The second dataset included incident cases in the period 1998–2002 (aged 20–65 years) diagnosed with schizophrenia (DSM-IV diagnostic codes 295, 297, 298, 299) and the same population control group (Drukker et al. submitted c). Multilevel logistic regression analyses enabled us to study service use rates controlled for individual-level demographic variables and socioeconomic status.

Crude analyses showed that all neighbourhood factors were associated with service use rates (all diagnoses, and diagnoses of schizophrenia only). In neighbourhoods that were worse off (socioeconomically deprived or low levels of social capital), rates were about 10–30 per cent higher. However, after controlling for individual-level demographic and socioeconomic factors, none of the neighbourhood factors was associated with service use. Thus, subjective measures of mental health are most responsive to neighbourhood factors, while effects on adults' treated psychiatric morbidity (if any) are not large enough to be demonstrated.

QUANTITY OF SERVICE CONSUMPTION IN ADULTS

Although rates of service consumption were not associated with any of the neighbourhood variables, the quantity of service consumption was. Total care consumption (i.e. intramural days in care + days in day care + outpatient contacts) and number of outpatient contacts (all patients) were higher in neighbourhoods with more informal social control (Drukker et al. 2004b). In addition, both socioeconomic deprivation and social cohesion and trust were associated with total care consumption, albeit statistically imprecise by conventional alpha. On the contrary, care consumption of patients with schizophrenia was not associated with any of these three neighbourhood variables (Drukker et al. submitted c). However, these patients used more psychiatric care when the neighbourhood was more residentially stable.

Although there was no association between informal social control and quantity of service consumption of patients diagnosed with schizophrenia, we think that the results studying all patients and studying the subgroup diagnosed with schizophrenia are in line. Residents of high-social-control neighbourhoods may monitor their psychiatric neighbours and contact mental health workers when needed. Thus, it can be argued that social capital induces patients to contact mental health services. Social capital is, theoretically, more available in residential stable neighbourhoods, explaining the association with quantity of service consumption of patients diagnosed with schizophrenia.

CHILDREN'S MENTAL HEALTH SERVICE USE

Mental health service consumption was also studied in children, using data from a case–control study (Gunther et al. 2003). The case–control data showed that children living in socioeconomically deprived neighbourhoods were more likely to come into contact with mental healthcare services (van der Linden et al. 2003). Furthermore, the effect of neighbourhood socioeconomic deprivation on mental health service use was stronger in neighbourhoods with lower levels of social cohesion and trust between residents.

Thus, social cohesion and trust mitigated the effects of socioeconomic deprivation in children. This mitigating effect was also reported in a study on changes in self-esteem between the ages of 11 years and 13–14 years (Drukker et al. submitted b) (see above). Thus, strong social cohesion and trust protected both against more serious mental health problems in all children and against lower levels of self-esteem in adolescents of higher-educated parents. This aspect of social capital may protect against the deleterious effects of neighbourhood socio-economic deprivation.

Results summarized

Almost all results of the MQoL evidenced that neighbourhood-level social capital was associated with quality of life and subjective mental health, both in adolescents and in adults (Drukker and van Os 2003; Drukker et al. 2003a, 2003b, submitted a). Informal social control may be most important for 11-year-olds' perceived mental health and behaviour and for 11-year-old boys' school achievement (Drukker et al. 2003a, submitted a), but this association was not found when the children were two to three years older (Drukker et al. submitted b).

In addition, social capital was not associated with adults' treated psychiatric morbidity (Drukker et al. 2004b, submitted c). However, strong social cohesion and trust mitigated the risk-increasing effect of socioeconomic deprivation in children (van der Linden et al. 2003). This mitigating effect of social cohesion and trust was also found when analysing changes in self-esteem between baseline and follow-up (Drukker et al. submitted b). Furthermore, our work did not support previous assumptions that social capital is on the pathway of effects of income inequality or residential instability (Drukker et al. 2004a, 2005a).

As described in our cross-national study, researchers should be cognisant of differences in the effects of social capital between different population groups within a city or between different cities in different countries or on different continents (Drukker et al. 2005b).

Pressing issues
Mechanisms of social capital

Several pathways have been suggested to explain why social capital impacts on quality of life and subjective mental health. First, both a more rapid diffusion of health information and the increased likelihood that healthy norms and behaviour are adopted might be responsible for a better health in high-social-capital neighbourhoods (Kawachi et al. 1999a). However, non-healthy norms and behaviour can also spread more easily in these neighbourhoods. This contradicts a simple positive relationship between social capital and healthy outcomes. Second, the association between social capital and (mental) health outcomes could be the result of environmental pollution. Socioeconomically deprived neighbourhoods usually are located in areas with environmental problems and pollution. Because socioeconomic deprivation and social capital are strongly associated (Drukker et al. 2003a), the environmental pollution in low-social-capital neighbourhoods could be responsible for non-specific effects on health and quality of life. For example, three deprived neighbourhoods in Maastricht are located near industrial areas; two others are near a highway and a railway. These five neighbourhoods were also low in social capital.

Finally, the association could be the result of psychological processes (Cullen and Whiteford 2001). Next to bonds within the family, bonds within the neighbourhood contribute to effective support and self-esteem, which may improve health (Kawachi et al. 1999a). In addition, people who feel in control of their everyday lives are more likely to take control of their health (McCulloch 2003). The last explanation may be the most plausible one, because it is in agreement with the follow-up results (Drukker et al. submitted b). These results showed that socioeconomic deprivation was associated with low self-esteem only if social cohesion and trust in the neighbourhood were low. Moreover, the present study found evidence that social capital was associated with subjective measures of health and quality of life, but not with objective outcomes (Drukker et al. 2003c), and that individual perceptions of social capital mediated the association between socioeconomic deprivation and quality of life (Drukker and van Os 2003). This underlines the importance of a subjective (psychological) component in the mechanism.

Context or composition?
Although social capital is a neighbourhood-level measure, measurement relies largely on the subjective information given by neighbourhood residents. The MQoL social capital measures were obtained from a sample of informants independent of the study sample. Nevertheless, answers of all informants are coloured by their individual characteristics. Using the PHDCN data, it has been shown that if the group of informants comprised a higher percentage of African Americans or unmarried people, had an older average age or had lower levels of socioeconomic status, then neighbourhood levels of mistrust (an aspect of social capital) were higher, and controlling for these characteristics substantially changed neighbourhood-level estimates (Subramanian et al. 2003). However, individual socioeconomic and demographic composition provide the basis for social interactions in a neighbourhood (Subramanian et al. 2003); therefore, controlling for individual characteristics leads to overadjustment. Fortunately, the authors also reported that raw social capital estimates and adjusted estimates were highly correlated (Subramanian et al. 2003). In addition, Maastricht respondents were more ethnically homogeneous. Therefore, although the MQoL used raw estimates of social capital only, it is highly likely that the findings are valid.

Furthermore, contextual effects have been defined as true neighbourhood effects, and compositional effects have been based on the individual characteristics of the residents of the neighbourhood (Cullen and Whiteford 2001; Pickett and Pearl 2001). Thus, controlling for individual-level characteristics would result in estimating true contextual effects. Compositional effects and contextual effects are interrelated and not mutually exclusive (Subramanian *et al.* 2003). For instance, people usually evaluate a neighbourhood before buying or renting a house there. So, theoretically, individuals with similar preferences and characteristics will concentrate in particular neighbourhoods. Because of this, even after controlling for known individual characteristics, neighbourhood-level associations may still be (partly) compositional.

This also implies that there is a possibility that residual confounding leads to spurious results at the neighbourhood level, because of 'omitted variable bias' (Leventhal and Brooks Gunn 2000). To put it more simply, families moving into or not moving out of neighbourhoods may differ from their peers in other things than the confounders that have been taken into account (e.g. motivation, literacy, etc.). This makes it even more difficult to discriminate between true contextual effects and true compositional effects.

The neighbourhood effects we measured are not related to the geography of the neighbourhood itself but to the people actually living there. These neighbourhood effects have both contextual and compositional components. Our research was not designed to distinguish between these. Hence, if policy interventions were to be based on our research, then ideally they would focus on the interaction between the neighbourhood and the people living there rather than trying to focus on each separately.

Level of measurement of social capital
The MQoL neighbourhoods were defined by the local authorities. They are widely used and ecologically meaningful geographical units. However, neighbourhood residents may perceive different boundaries to their neighbourhood. Until recently, no well-established method for using residents' definitions of neighbourhoods was available. Therefore, Coulton *et al.* (2001) conducted a pilot study in which 140 residents of several neighbourhoods were asked to draw what they believed were the boundaries of their neighbourhood. This pilot study reported clear variation between respondents. On average, the size of perceived neighbourhoods in square miles was similar to the size of defined neighbourhoods (i.e. census tracts, 2000–4000 residents). However, although the size was similar, boundaries were not.

The social capital questions used in the present study ask about direct neighbours and problems in the person's own street. Therefore, perceived neighbourhoods in the MQoL were assumed to be much smaller than defined neighbourhoods and were assumed to comprise only (part of) the street of the respondent and perhaps one or two side streets. This assumption is very different from the results presented by Coulton *et al.* (2001). In order to verify this assumption post hoc, the methods of Coulton *et al.* were applied in a relatively small convenience sample of colleagues and friends living in Maastricht ($n = 23$). Respondents were asked to draw what they would define as their neighbourhood on a map when thinking of the social capital questions (informal social control, social cohesion and trust). The maps showed that sizes of perceived neighbourhoods differed between the respondents, the smallest perceived neighbourhood being approximately 0.5 per cent of the defined neighbourhood and the largest perceived neighbourhood being approximately 75 per cent. Even the size of perceived neighbourhoods of two people living in the same house could differ by a factor of three. Although the size of the perceived neighbourhoods varied, all respondents drew their perceived neighbourhood boundaries within the boundaries of a defined neighbourhood, except for three respondents, of which one included a supermarket on the other side of the boundary and one included a recreational area.

Thus, since boundaries differ per person, perceived neighbourhoods cannot be used when studying neighbourhood-level social capital, and information must be aggregated to defined neighbourhoods. This is methodologically valid because boundaries of perceived neighbourhoods generally do not cross the boundaries of defined neighbourhoods. In addition, multilevel analyses showed that individual answers on informal social control and social cohesion and trust were grouped within defined neighbourhoods, and most outcome measures also showed statistically significant variation at (defined) neighbourhood level (σ_μ^2). In fact, the immeasurable perceived neighbourhoods were aggregated to larger neighbourhoods, and associations in smaller areas will be even larger than the reported associations. Thus, aggregating data to neighbourhood level is the best way in which to study neighbourhood social capital.

There is one exception: neighbourhood boundaries in the city centre follow relatively small streets, which, therefore, are less ecologically meaningful. Because none of the respondents lived near these boundaries, the boundaries in the city centre have to be excluded from the conclusion. Although it may be difficult to realize, it is recommended that future studies, using residents of neighbourhoods as informants on neighbourhood social capital, also include a question on the size and the boundaries of the perceived neighbourhoods. This will give more insight into the operational area of social capital.

Other methodological issues

The effects of social capital and socioeconomic deprivation could not be disentangled because of collinearity. In order to avoid this problem, future studies should stratify neighbourhoods by categories of socioeconomic deprivation and social capital and select the same number of neighbourhoods from each stratum.

Second, intra-class correlations were low in all multilevel regression models. However, most models did show statistically significant variation at neighbourhood level (σ_μ^2). In addition, neighbourhood researchers tend to analyse neighbourhood effects, even when the intra-class correlation and the neighbourhood variation are low, and it is generally held that this is warranted because effect sizes commonly viewed as large may translate into small proportions of variance (Raudenbush and Sampson 1999).

Finally, neighbourhood social capital may be beneficial not to every resident but only to mainstream group members (Cullen and Whiteford 2001; McKenzie et al. 2002). New immigrants entering a neighbourhood do not mix with the existing population (Flippen 2001), and minority children living in dissonant environments have lower levels of self-esteem than when living in a homogeneous consonant environment (Garcia Coll et al. 1996). Thus, minority members are exposed to the negative side of social capital, which may lead to lower levels of health and quality of life. More research specifically addressing minority groups is needed.

Implications

Although neighbourhood effects on treated psychiatric morbidity rates over and above individual differences could not be proven, all MQoL results showed consistently that social capital is associated with individual quality of life in adolescents and adults. Maastricht policy-makers could put more effort into enhancing social cohesion within (poor) neighbourhoods, next to interventions at the level of individual risk factors. However, increasing social capital will not be easy. In Boston, community participation in the neighbourhood Villa Victoria declined over two and a half decades, and policy-makers hired professional community organizers to increase residents' participation again, but the project failed (Small 2002). Policy-makers can provide the facilities, but success depends on the motivation of the residents. The authorities can only stimulate and encourage the residents to visit a community centre for activities.

Our results were presented to a group of social workers. They were surprised to learn that social capital was lower in socioeconomically deprived neighbourhoods. Usually, residents of poor neighbourhoods spend much time on the streets, while the streets in affluent neighbourhoods are rather empty. On the other hand, the results showed that residents of poor areas do not trust each other as much as residents of affluent areas do. In addition, residents of poor areas probably are used to perceive children getting into mischief, which results in lower levels of informal social control. Moreover, it is possible that they prefer not to get involved with other people's children, because they expect problems with either the children or their parents. The Maastricht social workers saw a task for themselves in teaching parents to accept that neighbours interfere with the behaviour of their children, because children, as they grow older, widen their activities beyond the range of parental control. This acceptance can be a first step in the process to enhance informal social control in poor neighbourhoods.

Furthermore, the reported interaction effect of residential instability supports a policy to improve the situation of residents of poor stable neighbourhoods. In these neighbourhoods, helping residents to find jobs could contribute to overcoming the feeling of being trapped in a desperate and hopeless situation (see pages 92–93). Social workers could use several strategies (Granovetter 1985). For example, they could cooperate with employment agencies in training and placement programmes and advocate changes in small-business regulations that put up barriers to legal entrepreneurship and self-employment. Second, they could stimulate social network factors of residents in job-search networking in the traditional and internet economies (Granovetter 1985).

Finally, as stated before, people usually evaluate a neighbourhood before buying or renting a house there. So, theoretically, individuals with similar preferences and characteristics will concentrate in particular neighbourhoods. In other words, similar person types tend to cluster in the same neighbourhood (social selection). This means that neighbourhood effects are not related to the geography of the neighbourhood itself but to the people actually living there. Therefore, interventions should focus on the interaction between the neighbourhood on the one hand and its residents on the other. Moving people to another neighbourhood in order to solve quality-of-life problems is no solution from the point of view of the analyses described above.

References

Albeda, W., Ginjaar, L., Mackenbach, J.P., *et al.* (2001) *Sociaal-economische gezondheidsverschillen verkleinen: eindrapportage en beleidsaanbevelingen van de programmacommissie SEGV-II.* The Hague: ZON.

Aneshensel, C.S., Sucoff, C.A. (1996) The neighborhood context of adolescent mental health. *Journal of Health and Social Behaviour 37*, 293–310.

Berlim, M.T., Mattevi, B.S., Fleck, M.P. (2003) Depression and quality of life among depressed brazilian outpatients. *Psychiatric Services 54*, 254.

Bourdieu, P. (1986) *Forms of Capital.* New York: Free Press.

Bruhn, J.G., Wolf, S. (1979) *The Roseto Story: An Anatomy of Health.* Norman, OK: University of Oklahoma.

Buka, S.L., Brennan, R.T., Rich-Edwards, J.W., Raudenbush, S.W., Earls, F. (2003) Neighborhood support and the birth weight of urban infants. *American Journal of Epidemiology 157*, 1–8.

CBS (Statistics Netherlands) (1996) *Landelijke wijk-en buurtindeling.* Voorburg: CBS.

CBS (Statistics Netherlands) *STATLINE 2003: CBS.* http://statline.cbs.nl/ (accessed 2 January 2003).

Coleman, J.S. (1990) Social capital. In J.S. Coleman (ed) *The Foundations of Social Theory.* Cambridge, MA: Harvard University Press.

Coulton, C.J., Korbin, J., Chan, T., Su, M. (2001) Mapping residents' perceptions of neighborhood boundaries: a methodological note. *American Journal of Community Psychology 29,* 371–383.

Croudace, T.J., Kayne, R., Jones, P.B., Harrison, G.L. (2000) Non-linear relationship between an index of social deprivation, psychiatric admission prevalence and the incidence of psychosis. *Psychological Medicine 30,* 177–185.

Cullen, M., Whiteford, H. (2001) *The Interrelations of Social Capital with Health and Mental Health.* Canberra: Commonwealth of Australia.

Dalgard, O.S., Tambs, K. (1997) Urban environment and mental health: a longitudinal study. *British Journal of Psychiatry 171,* 530–536.

De Vries, J., van Heck, G.L. (1995) *Nederlandse WHOQOL-100.* Tilburg: Tilburg University.

De Vries, J., Drent, M., van Heck, G.L., Wouters, E.F. (1998) Quality of life in sarcoidosis: a comparison between members of a patient organisation and a random sample. *Sarcoidosis, Vasculitis, and Diffuse Lung Diseases 15,* 183–188.

Diez Roux, A.V., Merkin, S.S., Arnett, D., *et al.* (2001) Neighborhood of residence and incidence of coronary heart disease. *New England Journal of Medicine 345,* 99–106.

Driessen, G., Gunther, N., van Os, J. (1998a) Shared social environment and psychiatric disorder: a multilevel analysis of individual and ecological effects. *Social Psychiatry and Psychiatric Epidemiology 33,* 12, 606–612.

Driessen, G., Gunther, N., Bak, M., van Sambeek, M., van Os, J. (1998b) Characteristics of early- and late-diagnosed schizophrenia: implications for first-episode studies. *Schizophrenia Research 33,* 27–34.

Drukker, M., van Os, J. (2003) Mediators of neighbourhood socioeconomic deprivation and quality of life. *Social Psychiatry and Psychiatric Epidemiology 38,* 12, 698–706.

Drukker, M., Kaplan, C.D., Feron, F.J.M., van Os, J. (2003a) Children's health-related quality of life, neighbourhood socio-economic deprivation and social capital: a contextual analysis. *Social Science and Medicine 57,* 5, 825–841.

Drukker, M., Feron, F.J.M., van Os, J. (2003b) Buurtkenmerken en Kwaliteit van Leven bij kinderen en volwassenen, contextuele analyses. *Tijdschrift Sociale Geneeskunde 81,* 1, 9–17.

Drukker, M., Gunther, N., Feron, F.J.M., van Os, J. (2003c) Social capital and mental health versus objective measures of health in the Netherlands. *British Journal of Psychiatry 183,* 2, 174.

Drukker, M., Feron, F.J.M., van Os, J. (2004a) Income inequality at neighbourhood level and health-related quality of life: a contextual analysis. *Social Psychiatry and Psychiatric Epidemiology 39,* 6, 457–463.

Drukker, M., Driessen, G., Krabbendam, L., van Os, J. (2004b) The wider social environment and mental health service use. *Acta Psychiatrica Scandinavica 110,* 2, 119–129.

Drukker, M., Kaplan, C.D., van Os, J. (2005a) Residential instability in socioeconomically deprived neighbourhoods, good or bad? *Health and Place 11,* 121–129.

Drukker, M., Buka, S.L., Kaplan, C.D., McKenzie, K., van Os, J. (2005b) Social capital and children's general health in different sociocultural settings. *Social Science and Medicine 61,* 185–198.

Drukker, M., Feron, F.J.M., van Os, J. (submitted a) Neighbourhood socioeconomic and social factors and school achievement in boys and girls?

Drukker, M., Kaplan, C.D., Schneiders, J., Feron, F.J.M., van Os, J. (submitted b) The wider social environment and changes in self-reported quality of life in the transition from late childhood to early adolescence.

Drukker, M., Driessen, G., Krabbendam, L., van Os, J. (submitted c) Schizophrenia risk and care consumption of patients in the neighbourhood social environment.

Flippen, C. (2001) Neighborhood transition and social organization: the white to Hispanic case. *Social Problems 48*, 3, 299–321.

Garcia Coll, C., Lamberty, G., Jenkins, R., McAdoo, H.P., Crnic, K., Wasik, B.H. *et al.* (1996) An integrative model for the study of developmental competencies in minority children. *Child Development 67*, 5, 1891–1914.

Granovetter, M. (1985) Economic action and social structure: the problem of embeddedness. *American Journal of Sociology 91*, 3, 481–510.

Gunther, N., Slavenburg, B., Feron, F.J.M., van Os, J. (2003) Childhood social and early developmental factors associated with mental health service use. *Social Psychiatry and Psychiatric Epidemiology 38*, 3, 101–108.

Henderson, S., Whiteford, H. (2003) Social capital and mental health. *Lancet 362*, 9383, 505–506.

Hill, K.G., Howell, J.C., Hawkins, J.D., Battin-Pearson, S.R. (1999) Childhood risk factors for adolescent gang membership: results from the Seattle Social Development Project. *Journal of Research in Crime and Delinquency 36*, 300–322.

Kalff, A.C., Kroes, M., Vles, J.S.H., Hendricksen, J.G.M., Feron, F.J.M., Steyaert, J.G.P. *et al.* (2001) Neighbourhood level and individual level SES effects on child problem behaviour: a multilevel analysis. *Journal of Epidemiology and Community Health 55*, 4, 246–250.

Katschnig, H., Freeman, H., Sartorius, N. (1997) *Quality of Life in Mental Disorders.* Chichester: John Wiley & Sons.

Kawachi, I., Kennedy, B.P., Lochner, K., Prothrow-Stith, D. (1997) Social capital, income inequality, and mortality. *American Journal of Public Health 87*, 9, 1491–1498.

Kawachi, I., Kennedy, B.P., Wilkinson, R.G. (1999a) *The Society and Population Health Reader: Income Inequality and Health.* New York: The New Press.

Kawachi, I., Kennedy, B.P., Wilkinson, R.G. (1999b) Crime: social disorganization and relative deprivation. *Social Science and Medicine 48*, 6, 719–731.

Kleinhans, R., Veldboer, L., Duyvendak, J.W. (2001) De gemengde wijk in internationaal perspectief. [The mixed neighbourhood in international perspective]. In R.P. Hortulanus, J.E.M. Machielse (eds) *Op het snijvlak van de fysieke en sociale leefomgeving [At the Cutting Edge of the Physical and Social Environment].* The Hague: Elsevier, pp.71–88.

Landgraf, J.M., Abetz, L., Ware, J.E., Jr (1996) *Child Health Questionnaire (CHQ): A User's Manual.* Boston, MA: the Health Institute, New England Medical Center.

Leventhal, T., Brooks Gunn, J. (2000) The neighborhoods they live in: the effects of neighborhood residence on child and adolescent outcomes. *Psychological Bulletin 126*, 2, 309–337.

Markowitz, F.E., Bellair, P.E., Liska, A.E., Liu, J.H. (2001) Extending social disorganization theory: modeling the relationships between cohesion, disorder, and fear. *Criminology 39*, 2, 293–320.

McCulloch, A. (2001) Social environments and health: cross sectional national survey. *British Medical Journal 323*, 208–209.

McCulloch, A. (2003) An examination of social capital and social disorganisation in neighbourhoods in the British household panel study. *Social Science and Medicine 56*, 7, 1425–1438.

McKenzie, K., Whitley, R., Weich, S. (2002) Social capital and mental health. *British Journal of Psychiatry 181*, 4, 280–283.

Nussbaum, M. (1993) The quality of life. In M. Nussbaum, A. Sen (eds) *The Quality of Life.* Oxford: Clarendon Press, p.453.

Orley, J., Saxena, S., Herrman, H. (1998) Quality of life and mental illness: reflections from the perspective of the WHOQOL. *British Journal of Psychiatry 172*, 291–293.

Ormel, J., Lindenberg, S., Steverink, N., Vonkorff, M. (1997) Quality of life and social production functions: a framework for understanding health effects. *Social Science and Medicine 45*, 7, 1051–1063.

Pickett, K., Pearl, M. (2001) Multilevel analyses of neighbourhood socioeconomic context and health outcomes: a critical review. *Journal of Epidemiology and Community Health 55*, 2, 111–122.

Putnam, R.D. (1993) Making democracy work. *Civic Traditions in Modern Italy.* Princeton, NJ: Princeton University Press.

Raat, H., Bonsel, G.J., Essink Bot, M.L., Landgraf, J.M., Gemke, R.J.B.J. (2002) Reliability and validity of comprehensive health status measures in children: the Child Health Questionnaire in relation to the Health Utilities Index. *Journal of Clinical Epidemiology 55*, 1, 67–76.

Raudenbush, S.W., Sampson, R.J. (1999) Ecometrics: toward a science of assessing ecological settings, with application to the systematic social observation of neighborhoods. In American Sociological Association (ed) *Sociological Methodology.* Boston, MA: Blackwell, p.1–41.

Ross, C.E., Reynolds, J.R., Geis, K.J. (2000) The contingent meaning of neighborhood stability for residents' psychological well-being. *American Sociological Review 65*, 4, 581–597.

Sampson, R.J. (1997) Collective regulation of adolescent misbehavior: validation results from eighty Chicago neighborhoods. *Journal of Adolescent Research 12*, 2, 227–244.

Sampson, R.J., Raudenbush, S.W., Earls, F. (1997) Neighborhoods and violent crime: a multilevel study of collective efficacy. *Science 277*, 5328, 918–924.

Sampson, R.J., Morenoff, J.D., Earls, F. (1999) Beyond social capital: spatial dynamics of collective efficacy for children. *American Sociological Review 64*, 5, 633–660.

Schaar, I., Ojehagen, A. (2003) Predictors of improvement in quality of life of severely mentally ill substance abusers during 18 months of co-operation between psychiatric and social services. *Social Psychiatry and Psychiatric Epidemiology 38*, 2, 83–87.

Schama, S. (1988) *The Embarrassement of Riches: An Interpretation of Dutch Culture in the Golden Age.* Berkeley, CA: University of California Press.

Sloggett, A., Joshi, H. (1994) Higher mortality in deprived areas: community or personal disadvantage? *British Medical Journal 309*, 6967, 1470–1474.

Small, M.L. (2002) Culture, cohorts, and social organization theory: understanding local participation in a Latino housing project. *American Journal of Sociology 108*, 1, 1–54.

Soobader, M.J., LeClere, F.B. (1999) Aggregation and the measurement of income inequality: effects on morbidity. *Social Science and Medicine 48*, 6, 733–744.

Spergel, I.A. (1992) Youth gangs: an essay review. *Social Service Review 66*, 121–140.

Subramanian, S.V., Lochner, K.A., Kawachi, I. (2003) Neighborhood differences in social capital: a compositional artifact or a contextual construct? *Health Place 9*, 1, 33–44.

Valdez, A. (2003) Toward a typology of contemporary Mexican American youth gangs. In L. Kontos, D. Brotherton, L. Barrios (eds) *Gangs and Society: Alternative Perspectives.* New York: Columbia University Press, pp.12–40.

van der Linden, J., Drukker, M., Gunther, N., Feron, F.J.M., van Os, J. (2003) Children's mental health service use neighbourhood socioeconomic deprivation and social capital. *Social Psychiatry and Psychiatric Epidemiology 38*, 9, 507–514.

van Os, J., Driessen, G., Gunther, N., Delespaul, P. (2000) Neighbourhood variation in incidence of schizophrenia: evidence for person-environment interaction. *British Journal of Psychiatry 176*, 243–248.

Ware, J.E., Jr, Gandek, B. (1998) Overview of the SF-36 Health Survey and the International Quality of Life Assessment (IQOLA) Project. *Journal of Clinical Epidemiology 51*, 11, 903–912.

World Health Organization (WHO) (1998) Development of the World Health Organization WHOQOL-BREF quality of life assessment. The WHOQOL Group. *Psychological Medicine 28*, 3, 551–558.

Wilkinson, R.G. (1997) Comment: income, inequality, and social cohesion. *American Journal of Public Health 87*, 9, 1504–1506.

Wulffraat, N., van der Net, J.J., Ruperto, N., Kamphuis, S., Prakken, B.J., Ten Cate, R. *et al.* (2001) The Dutch version of the Childhood Health Assessment Questionnaire (CHAQ) and the Child Health Questionnaire (CHQ). *Clinical and Experimental Rheumatology 19*, 4, (Suppl. 23), S111–115.

CHAPTER 6

Social capital and mental health in the urban south, USA

A quantitative study

Carey Usher

How do our civic connections affect our health? Are our social ties and social trust intertwined with our wellbeing? Do the resources we receive from friends and acquaintances and those resources we share with others help or hinder us in our day-to-day lives? How far can people extend themselves into their communities before their own resources are taxed? Furthermore, how does the structure of a community shape and mould the interactions and social networks of its residents? These questions are examined and answered in this chapter.

The concept of social capital, which connects our interactions and associations to our individual and community wellbeing and productivity, is examined as a unique and important social resource in the context of impoverishment and racial and economic segregation. Social capital has been found to increase quality-of-life indicators, such as feelings of optimism and life satisfaction, thus directly influencing the wellbeing of individuals and groups (Scheufele and Shah 2000). Missing from the current literature, however, are the ways in which social capital, as a social resource, mediates the effects of social stressors on mental wellbeing. Using a mediation model of wellbeing derived from the psychosocial resources approach to distress (Ensel and Lin 1991; LaGory *et al.* 1990; Lin and Ensel 1989), this chapter addresses how social capital mediates the effects of environmental and economic stressors on the mental wellbeing of impoverished residents and communities. On a broader scale, the ways in which ecological context affects social capital and wellbeing are examined.

Two sets of data were utilized to address these issues. The first consisted of over 200 cases collected from face-to-face interviews with household decision-makers in a low-income, mostly minority, inner-city neighbourhood in Birmingham, Alabama. The neighbourhood is severely impoverished and fits the conceptualization of a high-poverty ghetto: roughly 35 per cent of the population within the neighbourhood is below the poverty level, and 75 per cent is African American. Additionally, the neighbourhood exhibits the physical characteristics of a high-poverty ghetto: vacant and dilapidated housing, litter, broken glass, graffiti and broken-down cars (Jargowsky 1997; Wilson 1987).

The second dataset examined the Social Capital Community Benchmark Initiative (Saguaro Seminar 2000), which is comprised of 500 randomly selected respondents from several communities in the Birmingham metropolitan area of Alabama. Demographic characteristics of the Birmingham metropolitan area are drastically different compared with the neighbourhood sample. Racially, the metropolitan area is approximately 61 per cent white and 37 per cent African American. The median household income in 1989 was approximately US$26,000.

Descriptive statistics and multivariate regression analyses were used to investigate these data. The variables used in the analyses included sociodemographic background controls, neighbourhood characteristics and US census demographics, environmental stressors, economic stressors, social capital, and various outcome measures of mental wellbeing.

Importance of study

The strength of social ties, how these ties affect social networks and build social capital, and how these ties facilitate either social isolation or social integration are especially important for residents and communities within the urban system (Granovetter 1973; Lin et al. 1981; Thoits 1995). Neighbourhoods that are spatially distinct and segregated from other areas can lessen the likelihood of social isolation and alienation within them, while at the same time promoting cultural isolation and detachment from the larger community (LaGory and Pipkin 1981). If social groups are bounded spatially, then social networks tend to be bounded spatially. This segregation is functional for the urban system in the sense that it serves to alleviate much of the confusion caused by potential contact with dissimilar others in the inner city (LaGory and Pipkin 1981; Pipkin et al. 1983).

However, the cultural isolation that is caused by segregation may be unhealthy for the individual as well as for the neighbourhood as a whole (Logan and Molotch 1987; Ross et al. 2000). With spatially bounded social networks, communities may not have the resources available to promote organization and growth. Spatially bounded networks may also produce an absence of trust outside of the community. On the other hand, weak ties that bridge individuals to other communities can increase mobility opportunities, allow increased access to information, and facilitate social cohesion, thus activating a sense of community and increasing access to resources (Granovetter 1973; Putnam 2000).

In this study, the nature of social ties and associations and trust in the community was examined as they affect mental wellbeing. Adding trust to the conceptualization of social support and social networks includes an important subjective component to the investigation of social ties. Without trust, feelings of reciprocity between individuals who may be connected at either an informal or a formal level will not exist. Without reciprocity, information and resource exchange will not occur as often or as smoothly. Without this exchange, social capital will not exist. Past studies have focused either on social ties and associations or on levels of trust. However, to truly measure social capital, we should combine trust, social ties and social associations (Putnam 2000). The intentions of this investigation were to raise the study of social capital to a new level in sociological research and to add this important component of social interaction to research on the distress process.

Poverty and physical and mental health risks and hazards are distributed differently within cities, as are the social goods and services capable of protecting city residents from harm (Fitzpatrick and LaGory 2000). Strong organizational structures within an area have been found to protect individuals against hazard and risk and against stress and illness, but inner-city neighbourhoods often can be characterized by low levels of social organization (Fitzpatrick and LaGory 2000; LaGory and Pipkin 1981). With a lack of social organization, city residents may experience role segmentation and loss of close personal ties (LaGory and Pipkin 1981). Without cohesive social organization, neighbourhoods experience a decline in the prevalence and strength of social networks, in the degree of responsibility that individuals take for neighbourhood problems, and in the degree of participation in formal and voluntary organizations tied to the larger community (Fitzpatrick and LaGory 2000; Wilson 1996).

The links between the individual and the group are often seen as essential to the health of that individual as well as to the health of the social system, and individuals with substantial social networks have been found to have better physical health and lower mortality rates (Fitzpatrick and LaGory 2000). These social resources, most notably the social ties among neighbours, are some of the most important mediators of stressors such as neighbourhood disorganization and poverty on distress (Ross et al. 2000). However, the organization of one's social network often mirrors the organization of one's engagement with the larger community and society (Pearlin 1989), which may leave residentially segregated low-income minorities at a disadvantage.

Granovetter's (1973) definitive work on the benefits of establishing weak social ties shows the importance of developing social ties that link together members of different groups, rather than focusing on the development of strong ties that breed local cohesion. Strong ties tend to be concentrated within particular, often dense, spatially constrained groups. On the other hand, people or groups to whom individuals are tied weakly are more likely to move in different circles and have access to information that varies from what one would receive in a dense network. Additionally, weak ties increase mobility opportunities and bring together various networks, thus creating social cohesion and activating a sense of community. In the absence of these weak social ties, individuals can miss out on many crucial forms of resources and social supports that are not readily available within dense networks. However, Fitzpatrick and LaGory (2000) discussed the most powerful aspect of support for people who may not have extensive social networks as whether or not a person has an intimate, confiding relationship with another person. This aspect of support is a crucial mediator of distress. Given the likelihood of strong family ties within the local community (Brown *et al.* 1992), low-income African Americans may have access to this critical form of support.

The discussion of social support and wellbeing has been cast in a new light with the work of Putnam (2000) on social capital. Granovetter (1973) argued that the types of social ties that an individual develops, whether strong or weak, influence the resources that are available to that individual. Social capital, a product of human action, is argued to be the resource that emerges from one's social ties (Astone *et al.* 1999). Social capital consists of intra-community and extra-community ties that are actually or potentially productive in the achievement of certain ends (Astone *et al.* 1999; Flora 1998; Gargiulo and Benassi 2000). Social capital has several dimensions. These include the number of relationships with individuals or groups that a person has, the strength of those relationships, which involves the development of trust (Flora 1998), and the nature and amount of resources available as a result of those relationships (Astone *et al.* 1999; Gargiulo and Benassi 2000). The associational behaviours that have been identified by Guest and Lee (1983) to be critical for neighbourhood organization – informal neighbouring, formal relationships and social ties – and membership in formal and informal voluntary organizations are the same critical ingredients required in order to build social capital (Putnam 2000).

Social capital as a critical resource

Social capital assumes that individuals and groups can gain resources from their connections to one another. The core idea behind social capital is that social networks and supports have value (Putnam 2000), much like the values attributed to physical capital and human capital (Paxton 1999). The social contacts made within these networks affect the productivity and wellbeing of individuals and groups (Paxton 1999; Putnam 2000). When social capital is present, individual and group capacity for action is increased, production and cooperative social interaction are facilitated (Glaeser *et al.* 2000; Paxton 1999), a range of significant economic and political phenomena such as free-rider problems are influenced (Glaeser *et al.* 2000), atmospheres conducive to economic activity are produced, and the collective will to solve community problems is enhanced (Wilson 1997).

Portes (1998), in a critique of social capital, identified the positive as well as the negative aspects of social capital and its function in society. One benefit of social capital is that high levels of this resource can increase social control in an environment. Tight community networks can use social capital to promote compliance and maintain discipline without using formal or overt controls. Another benefit is that social capital creates familial support that primarily benefits children. Social capital of the family is embodied in the relationships between parents and children. When parents are an important part of their children's lives, intellectual development and socialization of children are heightened (Coleman 1988). A third benefit is through extra-familial networks, where ties and associations with other individuals and groups can help people to gain direct access to economic resources and valued credentials.

Portes (1998) also identified negative consequences of social capital. The first of these concerns the exclusion of outsiders. The same strong ties that bring benefits to members of a group commonly enable that group to bar others from access to the group and its benefits. The second consequence is that group or community closure may prevent the success of business initiatives by its members. The third negative consequence is that social capital may restrict individual freedom and autonomy. The fourth concerns downward leveling norms. Because in some situations group solidarity is cemented by a common experience of adversity, individual success stories of group members may undermine group cohesion. To remain cohesive, particular norms within the group may function to keep members in place rather than allowing them to achieve individual success.

Consideration of the advantages and disadvantages of social capital necessitates a closer look into the components of social capital and how social capital works. According to Paxton (1999), social capital involves two components: the objective associations between individuals and groups, and the subjective types of tie between individuals and groups. The objective associations refer to how individuals or groups are tied to each other in social space or the proximity of social ties. To create social capital, these ties will subjectively be reciprocal and trusting and involve positive emotion. Therefore, at a community level, positive social capital is expected to occur when there are positive trusting ties between individuals in different groups. On the other hand, social capital is expected to have negative effects when there is low between-group trust and networks but high within-group trust and networks. An intensely cohesive network without between-group ties has, in effect, built walls that block information and resource diffusion to other networks and bar integration of outside information and resources. It is important to keep in mind that there are circumstances when there is no social capital at all. When community members are extremely detached, there is no formal or informal association available to create positive or negative social capital. This absence of association can create social isolation, which is a stressor in itself (Thoits 1995). The objective types of ties that individuals and groups have are important in acquiring positive social capital, as is level of trust, which is the subjective component of social capital (Paxton 1999).

Summary of study

The questions posed in the introduction arose in response to the interest in social capital as a critical social resource in the wellbeing of individuals and of communities (Putnam 2000). I propose that social capital is a critical social resource on an individual and a community level. On the individual level, social capital, conceptualized as the density and extensity of social ties, levels of trust in individuals and in community, and level of engagement in instrumental and expressive voluntary organizations, will mediate the effects of environmental and economic stressors on the mental wellbeing of residentially segregated minorities in the inner city. On the community level, spatial characteristics including racial segregation and poverty will either promote or discourage the accumulation of social capital, which will in turn affect the wellbeing of community residents.

This chapter examines two distinct types of social capital and their relationships to the individual and the community. I will consider an individual's degree of social participation in various organizations and the extent of trust and social ties across socially diverse people. A social resource model of distress was used to address the question: how does social capital mediate the effects of environmental and economic stressors on the mental and physical wellbeing of residents of an impoverished neighbourhood?

After assessing personal economic and environmental stressors in an impoverished area and their effects on wellbeing and social resources, a second resource model was introduced, using poverty-related characteristics of place rather than personal stressors to examine the distress process and the role of social capital across different types of community. The goal of this second model was to examine how place affected wellbeing and resources, above and beyond the personal stressors faced by residents of impoverished areas. Several important patterns emerged from the analyses, and the following results show that the link between social capital and personal wellbeing is complex.

Place and wellbeing

The stress-related models of wellbeing used to answer the question 'Does place affect health?' used both individual perceptions of place-related poverty stressors and objective place-based characteristics as stressors. To determine the effects of poverty-related, individual-level stressors on wellbeing, I examined high-poverty area residents' perceptions of economic and environmental stress. As expected, the extent of economic stressors experienced by the individual was a significant predictor of mental distress. Mental distress was measured over the previous week using a combination of a modified version of the Centre for Epidemiological Studies' depression scale and three questions assessing anxiety. Economic stressor is an index constructed by a factor analysis of several economic variables; these include items such as skipping payments in the last six months in order to get by and worrying about debt. Individuals who experienced economic stressors reported higher levels of anxiety and depressive symptomatology than those with lower levels of economic stress. The experience of personal poverty increased mental distress.

Environmental stressors were conceptualized in this study as perceived and real neighbourhood disorder. Neighbourhood disorder can be assessed in part through examining the extent of territorial functioning in an area. A neighbourhood that has high levels of territorial functioning is one in which residents take special care in the maintenance of their homes and environment. Lawns are groomed, flowers are planted, pavements are kept clean and homes are maintained structurally and aesthetically in neighbourhoods with territorial functioning. The visible order of the neighbourhood encourages cooperative behaviours and trust within the community. Neighbourhoods with low levels of territorial functioning are visibly different from those with higher levels of territorial functioning, and life within these neighbourhoods is experienced differently. The sociability and trust of residents decline as the neighbourhood deteriorates. A lack of territorial functioning leads to disorder in the community and can isolate and alienate community residents. The extent of an individual's perceptions of neighbourhood disorder was found to significantly affect mental distress: people who experienced their neighbourhood as disordered reported higher levels of mental distress.

The next step in the study was to examine the objective place-based effects of neighbourhoods on individual wellbeing. Fitzpatrick and LaGory (2000) have identified several ecological factors that influence the wellbeing of residents of impoverished communities. These factors arise from the physical character of the community rather than from individual impoverishment. They include the presence of health hazards, economic and racial segregation, the degree of access that the population has to other areas, the level of resources contained in the space, and the extent of territorial functioning within the area. This study used the extent of economic and racial segregation to define neighbourhoods as disadvantaged. Disadvantaged neighbourhoods were defined as census tracts that were over 85 per cent minority and over 30 per cent below poverty. The intent of this measurement was to capture the stress related to contextual poverty rather than the personal poverty experienced by the individual. The analyses employed in this examination tested a place-based approach to emotional and physical wellbeing.

Situational self-efficacy, which is the feeling that the individual can make a positive impact on life in the community, was the emotional wellbeing outcome measure assessed in the examination of neighbourhood disadvantage. Descriptive statistics showed that roughly 66 per cent of the residents of the high-poverty area felt they could have an impact on making their community a better place to live, compared with almost 80 per cent of the respondents in the larger metropolitan area. This difference could be considered to suggest that the type of neighbourhood in which an individual lives affects their feelings of self-efficacy. However, the study is cross-sectional, and so only an association – not a causation – has been demonstrated. Although variation existed, the results of the analysis did not support the expectation that place-based characteristics affected self-efficacy. This finding was unexpected but positive, in that residents of disadvantaged and more affluent neighbourhoods alike appear to have access to this indicator of emotional wellbeing. Feelings of self-efficacy may be distributed unevenly in the population, but they do not appear to be affected by the contextual factors of impoverished areas. Equal access has positive implications for the individual as well as for the community at large. Especially important in impoverished neighbourhoods, feelings that one can have a positive impact on life in the community can lead to cooperation and trust in neighbours, which is necessary in order for improvements to be made.

Poverty, place and social capital

Within the high-poverty area, neither economic nor environmental stressors significantly affected individual social capital. This finding was unexpected but is an important indicator of the practicality of this social resource for impoverished individuals. Regardless of whether individuals experienced these stressors, they could still effectively engage in community participation and activity. Additionally, bonding social capital was not affected by residence in a disadvantaged community. Those who lived in disadvantaged areas and those in more affluent areas were equally likely to participate. This suggests that the characterization of high-poverty areas as disorganized and promoting social isolation is not uniformly true.

Another interesting aspect of participation was that although personal and contextual impoverishment did not appear to influence the extent of an individual's activities, race did. Within the impoverished community, African American respondents were significantly more likely to participate in neighbourhood activities than were white respondents. Conversely, within the metropolitan area, where African Americans were the numeric minority, white respondents were more likely to participate. This finding suggested that minority status did influence the extent of an individual's connections within the community. White residents of predominantly minority communities may be socially isolated within such communities, and minority members within predominantly white communities may experience that same isolation.

This variation in participation by racial dissimilarity probably can be attributed to levels of trust in neighbours. Trust of neighbours, which can be considered reflective of bridging social capital, was found to be disproportionately high in the high-poverty neighbourhood studied, with 71 per cent of the respondents reporting trust in their neighbours. Nationally, only 21 per cent of African Americans said they trusted their neighbors (Saguaro Seminar 2000). When people are more trusting of others, they are more likely to participate in the community (Putnam 2000). The variation between the trust levels of African Americans in this high-poverty neighbourhood and the national trust level suggested that racial homogeneity in a community may lead to higher levels of trust and, perhaps, higher levels of participation. That is not to say that all high-minority, high-poverty areas will have such levels of trust. Pipkin *et al.* (1983) suggested that the level of income and ethnic diversity in an area will be highly related to trust levels. The neighbourhood examined here is indeed relatively diverse for the so-called high-poverty ghetto characterizations.

Bridging social capital was conceptualized as the extent of social ties with dissimilar others and levels of trust in neighbours and community. This social resource is expected to assist individuals in 'getting ahead' (Putnam 2000) by providing access to a diversity of resources and information diffusion. Like participation, this resource was not affected by economic stressors or by the contextual aspects of disadvantaged neighbourhoods. However, bridging social capital was affected negatively by the experience of environmental stressors. Those individuals who perceived their neighbourhood as disordered were less likely to be tied socially to diverse others and were less likely to be trusting of others. This finding is especially important when considering the aspects of neighbourhood organization that promote trust and cooperation.

The discussion thus far has supported the critical idea that place matters for the wellbeing of individuals. Not only did personal experience of economic and environmental stressors affect wellbeing but also the context of the environment affected wellbeing. These poverty-related stressors were found to have less effect, however, on social capital. Social capital appeared to have a more complex dynamic with impoverishment than that found for other types of psychosocial resources. Neither participation nor bridging social capital was affected by contextual stressors, and personal experience of environmental stressors affected only bridging social capital.

Social capital and wellbeing

Social capital has been billed as a resource capable of solving a multitude of social problems (Putnam 2000). However, elaboration of the complexity and contrariness of social capital by Portes (1998), as well as variations between social capital and other psychosocial resources, suggest that social capital may not be a quick fix for societal ills. The following discussion explores the effects of social capital on individual mental wellbeing to determine whether this supposed resource is, in fact, resourceful.

For individuals residing in the inner city, where people are constantly struggling to make ends meet and avoid the hazards of a risky environment, participation was expected to be a critical asset assisting people in 'getting by'. The results showed a surprisingly more complex picture of social capital. Indeed, social capital can help as well as hinder individual wellbeing. Social ties born through participation were expected to decrease mental distress. Theoretically, these ties lead to asset networks, critical forms of support and mutual obligations within the community. They increase cohesiveness and create a sense of unity and collective problem-solving behaviours. The data indicated, however, that, in the case of mental wellbeing, such connections were not only asset networks but also webs of obligation. Instead of reducing distress, the extent of participation in various organizations actually tended to be associated with higher distress. Because many of the organizations that residents participated in were located within their community, it may be that these voluntary ties further burdened individuals already struggling with their own environmental and economic stressors. The obligations of time and energy required of the active participant in the inner city may simply serve as another source of stress, rather than as a mediator of the stress process.

The finding that participation was associated with increased mental distress may be considered to support Burt's (1997) structural hole theory; cohesive social ties are a source of rigidity within a social network. Although these civic connections may facilitate trust and cooperation between the individuals involved, these connected individuals often have little autonomy within these relationships and may, in fact, suffer rather than benefit from overobligation and network closure. Obligations in bonding relationships are mutual, and a person with large networks of these relationships and who experiences high levels of obligation can easily become socially overloaded or 'overcapitalized' (Vaux 1988), thus leading to higher levels of anxiety and depressive symptoms. Moreover, the reciprocation within relationships may be imbalanced, especially in an impoverished community. That participation actually increased levels of mental distress in this impoverished community should lead to a questioning and examination of the popular idea that social capital is a fast remedy to social problems and personal ills.

The effects of participation on mental wellbeing were not all negative. In the analysis of the metropolitan area, participation was found to be a very significant predictor of self-efficacy. People who were more involved in their communities appraised their personal potential to affect positive change in their neighbourhoods much higher than those who did not participate. Although this high appraisal of efficacy may indeed place even more burden on the mental wellbeing of the individual due to personal pressures on the self to be active, it suggests that communities that have a high density of civic connections will be healthier than those with fewer civic connections.

If self-efficacy is influenced by past success and failure, then the assumption can be made that people with high levels of self-efficacy have experienced past success rather than failure. In this case, self-efficacy was specific to the belief that the individual had the capacity to make the community a better place to live. The results showed that participation increased self-efficacy. Therefore, participation in the community increased the individual's belief that he or she could make the community a better place to live. Because self-efficacy is also influenced by the experience of success (Eden and Kinnar 1991), it could be argued that people who participate in the community will, in fact, work to make the community a better place to live and that this work can enhance community wellbeing.

Participation thus appeared to be a mixed blessing. Whereas extensive participation in the community may increase individual levels of mental distress, it could also serve to increase the overall health of the community itself.

Is bridging social capital or the extent of our social ties essential to our wellbeing? Is this 'resource' important for wellbeing even in areas that suffer severe limitations in other forms of capital? The answer to this question is a strongly supported and absolute 'yes'. Do the resources that we receive from friends and acquaintances and those resources that we share with others help or hinder us in our day-to-day lives? In every model examined in this study, bridging social capital, which is the extent of social ties with and trust in a diversity of others, was a significant predictor of wellbeing. People with diverse ties and trust in others were mentally healthier and had stronger feelings of self-efficacy compared with people with low levels of bridging social capital. This aspect of social capital is considered by Putnam (2000) to assist individuals in 'getting ahead'. In the case of individual wellbeing, this idea was supported strongly. Bridging social capital is, thus, a key asset and useful for the development of healthy individuals across different types of community.

An expansive body of literature focuses on social support and its effects on wellbeing. It tends, however, to examine only one form of support – perceived strong social tie support from family and confidants. These ties have been found repeatedly to offer the highest level of support. Although these strong ties are obviously important for wellbeing, this study showed that weak bridging ties were also very important for wellbeing, and true benefits from social capital stem from the contacts created through bridging across diverse individuals and groups. Within poor minority communities specifically, bridging ties are necessary to break the social and economic isolation produced by segregation.

The results of this study have shown that individual participation in the community and bridging social capital have significant effects, both positive and negative, on wellbeing in an impoverished community and in the general metropolitan area examined. The next goal of the study was to determine how the stressors associated with personal impoverishment and those associated with residence in an impoverished area interacted with social capital in affecting wellbeing. Did social capital mediate the effects of stressors on wellbeing? The results showed that social capital played a minor mediating role within the impoverished community. Additionally, social capital had no apparent effect on the stress associated with residence in a disadvantaged neighbourhood.

The overarching pattern found in this study was that, for low-income minority communities in particular, social capital may be more important as a communal resource than as a personal resource. The ties that bind people together in the face of impoverishment gave some modest comfort to those connected individuals, but in this case the ties that bind appeared to require much from the active community participant. Although healthy for the community itself, exchange in relationships among the poor is often one-sided, creating more obligation than benefit for the active giver.

Although these findings show that a high degree of participation in the community negatively impacts mental wellbeing, I do not conclude that people should stop their participation. Rather, individuals who have the time and resources to commit to the community should focus their energies on the activities and goals they can most accomplish. Instead of spreading already limited resources over a multitude of groups and community activities, individuals should concentrate their resources into groups that can gain the most from their resources as well as offer benefits to the active giver. Participation is an important form of social capital, but the obligations created through this social resource should be examined and understood before the initial investment by the individual. Ties that bridge, on the other hand, appeared to be beneficial for the individual.

Implications for the future

A conference held in Birmingham, Alabama, hosted over 200 non-profit organizations with the intent of learning about 'building community together' (Nonprofit Resource Center of Alabama 2001). The goal of this conference, and many others like it, was to discover how the problems of communities can be resolved through the building of and investment in social capital. Putnam (2000) has argued that social capital, which comprises our social networks and our capacity for trust and reciprocity, has been depleted over the past several years. His work suggests that social capital has important implications for community-level growth, such as better performance of government institutions, faster economic growth and less crime and violence, and that social capital increases individual happiness, healthiness and life expectancy. The results of this study supported the hypotheses that social capital is, indeed, a social resource that in some circumstances can combat stressors and increase wellbeing; however, there are also negative consequences of overcapitalization.

With the sudden popularity of the concept of social capital and the increase in grassroots organizations and non-profit groups attempting to maximize social capital on a community level, it is of great importance that the various forms of social capital and their effects on individuals and communities be understood. Particularly in underprivileged areas, where resources are already scarce, the limitations of social capital's utility should be analysed fully before interventions are introduced to increase community participation and activity. According to this study, overcapitalization in an underprivileged community has negative consequences for the mental wellbeing of its residents. Although community embeddedness may have positive implications for the cohesion of the community, it may also serve to isolate connected members from outside resources. This study confirms that bridging ties and trust in diverse others are very important social resources, and, for a community with tight internal bonding, these bridging ties are difficult to realize.

The study suggests that it may be far more important for bridging social capital to be the goal of community-level organizations interested in improving the health of people and of society. This study shows that place of residence and social capital in some circumstances can have negative consequences for the health of the individual. A community overcapitalized in bonding ties, and yet undercapitalized in bridging ties, may appear to be healthy and integrated on the surface, but such ties could signal heavy obligations rather than balanced exchange networks. The link between social capital and personal wellbeing is more complicated than the current popular perspective would have us believe, and the inconsistencies in the utility of social capital should be fully examined and understood before important investments are made.

What is clear from this study is that bridging social ties are important in the maintenance of individual and community wellbeing. Neighbourhood associations, non-profit and grassroots organizations, churches, schools and neighbours can all benefit from this knowledge by reaching out to diverse others and by encouraging the development and maintenance of these social ties. Those groups who take the responsibility of improving communities and neighbourhoods, i.e. the neighbourhood associations, the non-profit groups and the grassroots organizations, can and should lead this bridging by collaborating with other groups that are working towards the same goals. Bridging and sharing resources, information and even goals can serve the community in a more comprehensive fashion than small groups attempting to effect change alone. Thus, this research not only points out the problematic issues regarding individual investment in social capital and the benefits and disadvantages of social capital for wellbeing but also gives instructions for building healthy social networks among the groups.

References

Astone, N.M., Nathanson, C.A., Schoen, R., Kim, Y.J. (1999) Family demography, social theory, and investment in social capital. *Population Development Review 25*, 1–31.

Brown, D.R., Gary, L.E., Greene, A.D., Milburn, N.G. (1992) Patterns of social affiliation as predictors of depressive symptoms among urban blacks. *Journal of Health and Social Behavior 33*, 242–253.

Burt, R.S. (1997) The contingent value of social capital. *Administrative Science Quarterly 42*, 339–365.

Coleman, J. (1988) Social capital in the creation of human capital. *American Journal of Sociology 94*, 95–120.

Eden, D., Kinnar, J. (1991) Modeling Galatea: boosting self-efficacy to increase volunteering. *Journal of Applied Psychology 76*, 770–780.

Ensel, W.M., Lin, N. (1991) The life stress paradigm and psychological distress. *Journal of Health and Social Behavior 32*, 321–341.

Fitzpatrick, K., LaGory, M. (2000) *Unhealthy Places: The Ecology of Risk in the Urban Landscape.* New York: Routledge.

Flora, J.L. (1998) Social capital and communities of place. *Rural Sociology 63*, 481–506.

Gargiulo, M., Benassi, M. (2000) Trapped in your own net? Network cohesion, structural holes, and the adaptation of social capital. *Organization Science 11*, 183–196.

Glaeser, E.L., Laibson, D.I., Scheinkman, J.A., Soutter, C.L. (2000) Measuring trust. *Quarterly Journal of Economics August*, 811–846.

Granovetter, M.S. (1973) The strength of weak ties. *American Journal of Sociology 78*, 1360–1380.

Guest, A.M., Lee, B.A. (1983) The social organization of local areas. *Urban Affairs Quarterly 19*, 217–240.

Jargowsky, P. (1997) *Poverty and Place: Ghettoes, Barrios and the American City.* New York: Russell Sage.

LaGory, M., Pipkin, J. (1981) *Urban Social Space.* California, CA: Wadsworth Publishing.

LaGory, M., Ritchey, F.J., Mullis, J. (1990) Depression among the homeless. *Journal of Health and Social Behavior 31*, 87–101.

Lin, N., Ensel, W.M. (1989) Life stress and health: stressors and resources. *American Sociological Review 54*, 382–399.

Lin, N., Ensel, W.M., Vaughn, J.C. (1981) Social resources and strength of ties: structural factors in occupational status attainment. *American Sociological Review 46*, 393–405.

Logan, J.R., Molotch, H.L. (1987) *Urban Fortunes: The Political Economy of Place.* Berkeley, CA: University of California Press.

Nonprofit Resource Center of Alabama (2001) 2001 Nonprofit Summit: Building Community Together. 26 April 2001, Birmingham, Alabama.

Paxton, P. (1999) Is social capital declining in the United States? A multiple indicator assessment. *American Journal of Sociology 105*, 88–127.

Pearlin, L.I. (1989) The sociological study of stress. *Journal of Health and Social Behavior 30*, 241–256.

Pipkin, J., LaGory, M., Blau, J.R. 1983 *Remaking the City: Social Science Perspectives on Urban Design.* Albany, NY: State University of New York Press.

Portes, A. (1998) Social capital: its origins and applications in modern sociology. *Annual Review of Sociology 24*, 1–24.

Putnam, R. (2000) *Bowling Alone: The Collapse and Revival of American Community.* New York: Simon and Schuster.

Ross, C.E., Reynolds, J., Geis, K. (2000) The contingent meaning of neighbourhood stability for resident's psychological well-being. *American Sociological Review 65*, 581–597.

Saguaro Seminar (2000) *The Social Capital Benchmark Survey.* Cambridge, MA: Harvard University, Kennedy School of Government.

Scheufele, D.A., Shah, D.V. (2000) Personality strength and social capital: the role of dispositional and informational variables in the production of civic participation. *Communication Research 27*, 107–131.

Thoits, P. (1995) Stress, coping, and social support processes: where are we, what next? *Journal of Health and Social Behavior* Spec. No. 53–79.

Vaux, A. (1988) *Social Support: Theory, Research, and Intervention.* New York: Praeger.

Wilson, W.J. (1987) *The Truly Disadvantaged: The Inner-City, the Under Class, and Public Policy.* Chicago, IL: University of Chicago Press.

Wilson, W.J. (1996) *When Work Disappears: The World of the New Urban Poor.* New York: Vintage.

Wilson, P.A. (1997) Building social capital: a learning agenda for the twenty-first century. *Urban Studies 34*, 745–760.

CHAPTER 7

Social capital and mental health of women living in informal settlements in Durban, South Africa, and Lusaka, Zambia

Liz Thomas

Introduction

Social determinants of health are receiving increasing attention in the literature (Marmot and Wilkinson 1999) and have a raised international profile through the establishment of the World Health Organization (WHO) Commission on Social Determinants of Health in 2005. Social capital has become a new lens through which to explore health outcomes in tandem with a range of disciplines, such as political science (Putnam 2000) and economics (Serageldin and Grootaert 2000).

The exploration of the interface of social capital and mental health outcomes provides a new opportunity to explore mental health and community social resources. This interface is especially important in the case of developing countries, where, due to limited resources, development and public health concerns are prioritized while mental health issues are often marginalized.

Increasing mental health burden in developing countries

Mental health is increasingly on the international health agenda as '... WHO strives to shift mental health from the periphery to a more prominent position in global public health' (WHO 2001). In developing countries, mental health has been seen as a relatively unimportant health issue by national governments, given the context of the growing challenge of poverty. However, the WHO estimates that developing countries are expected to bear a disproportionate burden in the anticipated increase in mental ill-health (WHO 2001). Morbidity due to mental ill-health is higher in women than men (Patel *et al.* 1999). In developing countries, the increase in the burden of mental ill-health, and common mental disorders in particular, is understood in part as a response to the pressures of change, conflict and urbanization (Harpham and Blue 1995a) and the impact of human immunodeficiency virus (HIV)/acquired immune deficiency syndrome (AIDS) (Webb 1999).

Although there has been an increasing emphasis on the importance of mental health by the WHO, this health priority was not translated into the Millennium Development Goals (MDGs) and mental health has not been considered in development debates. The international development agenda for the new millennium focused on general health deliverables, such as reducing the infant mortality rate and increasing access to potable water, which are likely to impact on mortality outcomes. Mental health has not been given adequate consideration in developing countries, where mortality rates are high because improved mental health results in reduced morbidity rather than reduced mortality. Nevertheless, neuropsychiatric disorders account for nearly one-third of disability in the world when measured by disability-adjusted life-years (WHO 2001) and in the region of 18 per cent of disability in Africa. Further, there is a complex and dynamic relationship between poverty and psychological health (Patel *et al.* 1999).

The development debates have not directly taken cognisance of mental health, but the mental health of communities has an indirect impact on development outcomes. One of the key principles in development discourse since the late 1980s has been the focus on community participation. The MDGs are underpinned by a rights-based approach in terms of which the participation by all stakeholders and beneficiaries is seen as critical (United Nations 2001). This approach assumes that communities are able and willing to participate in local development initiatives. This chapter argues that an understanding of the mental health and social capital of communities provides valuable insights for the design of community participation initiatives in developing countries.

Social capital as a potential resource in urban contexts in developing countries

Cities in southern Africa have experienced rapid urbanization during the past 30 years. The populations of major urban areas have expanded faster than the capacity of local government to provide access to land, housing, basic services (water and sanitation) and healthcare. Areas of informal settlements have mushroomed and city governments have not been able to mobilize resources for the development and upgrading of informally settled areas. In the context of slowing economies, rural to urban migrants have struggled to generate sufficient income to get ahead. In addition to income, another resource is that of social capital. One of the ideas promoted in the development literature has been that social capital could be a resource to help communities get ahead. Serageldin and Grootaert (2000) refer to social capital as 'the glue that holds societies together'. Social capital has been identified as a resource for development (Woolcock 1998), a resource to help communities not only to 'get by' but also to 'get ahead' (de Souza Briggs, quoted in Putnam 2000, p.23). In a context of poverty, some have raised concerns about the degree to which social resources in the community can be mobilized (Beall 2000) and whether expecting communities to address their own problems is an abdication of responsibility by the state and international funders (Fine 2001).

Social capital has been disaggregated in a number of ways into component parts. One such disaggregation is that of structural and cognitive social capital (Bain and Hicks 1998), as described in Chapter 1. From a public health perspective, cognitive social capital could be considered primarily to be a factor impacting on individual health outcomes, while structural social capital could impact on community health and wellbeing. Not surprisingly, the links between structural and cognitive social capital have been rightly described by McKenzie *et al.* (2002, p.280) as 'complex and multidimensional'.

Study focus

This chapter draws on research undertaken in Lusaka, Zambia, and Durban, South Africa, and explores the social capital of women in these communities, their mental health and their involvement in development activities. The findings point towards the importance of those involved in development initiatives to be cognisant of the factors that limit vulnerable people in the community participating and the opportunity to address mental ill-health through development and empowerment projects.

Method

The data for the analysis are drawn from research in two informal settlements, selected as being typical of low-income residents in Durban and Lusaka. A two-phase random sample of 250 women aged between 16 and 40 years was selected. Quantitative data were collected on the sociodemographic profile of each participant and her household, on social capital using an adapted version (Harpham *et al.* 2002) of the World Bank Social Capital Assessment Tool (Krishna and Shrader 1999), on the woman's health (self-rated health and mental health using the Self-Reporting Questionnaire 20, SRQ20 (WHO 1994)). The SRQ20 instrument is a 20-question self-administered questionnaire requiring the respondent to answer yes or no to having experienced various indicators of mental distress during the past month. This instrument has become an internationally validated screening tool for mental distress and makes use of a locally determined cut-off on the 20-question scale. The appropriate cut-offs for Lusaka and Durban were based on previous studies in Zambia and South Africa (Aidoo 1998; Webb 1999). The questionnaire survey was conducted by women who spoke the local languages. The results from the survey were explored further in focus groups.

Objectives of the study

In a context of the anticipated increase in the rate of mental ill-health in developing countries and the high proportion of recent women migrants living in informal settlements in large urban areas, it was anticipated that women living in informal areas would be more vulnerable to mental ill-health. The research was undertaken with the expectation that there would be a relationship between the mental health of women living in informal settlements and the social and physical context in which they lived. The aim *inter alia* was to explore the associations between their health and the social and physical environment with a view to being able to inform health and development policy.

Study context

Zambia and South Africa have been through major transformations politically. Zambia gained independence in the 1960s, while South Africans struggled for and claimed democracy in 1994. South Africa's strong local civic mobilization leading up to the first democratic elections was expected to present a very different social capital profile for women compared to those in Zambia, who had not fought for their rights or experienced rapid political transformation. The study sites were selected to capture similar socioeconomic conditions for comparative purposes. The women in both settlements were found to be very poor. The majority had low levels of education and limited sources of income. Each settlement had similar levels of development, with limited access to basic services such as water supply, sanitation and electricity. The settlements had very different social histories leading to their growth. Although the majority of women in both settlements were new residents (three-quarters of the sampled group in both settlements had lived in the area for five years or less), they had very different migration histories. The women in Lusaka were largely recent migrants from rural areas of Zambia who had come to the settlement as 'new wives'. In contrast, the majority of the women living in the settlement in Durban had moved into the area from other settlements in the city. Despite the common elements between the two groups (low-income women living in poorly serviced urban settlements), there were differences in the profiles of the women's health, mental health and social capital.

Study findings

The characteristics of group membership and the extent of civic activity, two key indicators of social capital, highlight that there appeared to be very little glue that kept the communities together or structural elements that facilitated mutually beneficial collective action. Neither of the settlements had a strong community development committee or a powerful delivery-focused local leadership structure.

Participation of women in groups

In Lusaka, the types of group operating in the area were almost exclusively church groups. Four out of five (80%) women belonged to church groups that operated in the community. The groups performed a range of social support and welfare functions, including helping new migrants to adjust to urban life and to 'respect' their husbands. In Durban, church groups were found to be the dominant type of group that women had membership of, and very few other groups existed. Half of the women in Durban belonged to a church group. In contrast to the existence of locally based church groups in Lusaka, the churches the women in Durban belonged to operated outside of the settlement, in areas where the women had previously resided. The church groups that the women in Durban belonged to thus did not contribute to the sense of community in the settlement where they actually lived.

The differences in the range of functions performed by the groups and in the membership patterns between the settlements should be understood in the context of the history of the settlement and the sociopolitical context of each city. In both cases, three-quarters (75%) of the women had lived in the settlement for five years or less. Given the relative newness of the establishment of the settlements and the recent immigration by the women interviewed, it was expected that the structural social capital would be somewhat limited. In the case of Lusaka, the majority of women had recently moved from rural areas to the urban area because of marriage. The church groups functioned to help them assimilate and became an instant 'community', but not without the sanction of the rules of how to treat one's husband through the *chinai* groups of the church. Single women were excluded from membership of these church groups. Although the majority (75%) of the women in Durban had also settled in the area in the previous five years, they had moved from other settlements in the city to the new area. The long-standing intra-urban migration patterns in Durban (Cross *et al.* 1992) meant that the women (the 50% who were members of groups) had already established relationships with churches, women and family in other areas of the city.

In both cases, the contribution of the church groups was primarily to provide social support and a sense of belonging. In these cases, group membership could be understood as contributing to the cognitive social capital of the women rather than structural social capital. Noticeable by their absence were groups operating in the community focused on community-level outcomes (Uphoff's mutually beneficial collective action). In the absence of other groups such as development committees, local church groups may well be an avenue through which local community-development-focused initiatives could operate. It is important to understand the local context, as a church-group-focused approach may be appropriate in places like the settlement in Lusaka but would not be possible where church groupings are not based locally, as in Durban.

Participation of women in civic activities

Despite the very different sociopolitical developments in the previous decade between the two settlements, the level of civic involvement by women in both contexts was very limited. It was expected that the women living in the settlement in Durban would have reported some involvement in local political activities. This was anticipated, given the relatively recent political transformation in South Africa (in 1994), the politicization of urban areas in particular, recent local government elections and prominence given to the promotion of women's rights nationally and in local development initiatives. The findings show that other than having voted in the elections, the women in Durban and Lusaka had hardly participated in any local political or civic activities. Reasons that emerged from the focus group included: 'generally membership in most groups has gone down. For example, the credit club for women is now smaller because most women cannot afford to make contributions' (Lusaka).

Where groups are set up to address community issues, 'wherever there was any benefit to the members of the group, men were always excluding women' (Durban). Women were also excluded because 'women's voices were not heard by the men' (Durban).

Not surprisingly, in Lusaka, half the women felt that they had no influence on decisions that affected their area, and more than two-thirds (71%) had not participated in identified civic activities. In Durban, other than having voted, more than two-thirds (70%) of the women had not participated in any other civic activities, and less than a fifth thought that they could influence decisions in their area. Comments from the focus groups in Durban point to some of the underlying reasons: 'Attendance at community meetings is poor, people are sick and tired of promises.' 'It is pointless to attend these meetings because we are not given a chance to express ourselves.'

The limited extent to which women are involved in community-level activities that impact on their living conditions appears to be a function of their impressions about the marginal power they have to influence decisions. This points to the need to target development initiatives to empower women, building on the confidence of women who believe that they can influence things. Particular attention is needed to promote the participation of women in meaningful community decision-making, where their involvement will have positive impact.

Having provided an overview of group membership and participation in civic activities as two social capital indicators, it is appropriate to ask whether there was an association between social capital indicators and the health (and mental health) of the women.

The women's self-reported mental health

Between one-third and one-half of the women interviewed showed signs of poor mental health (using the SRQ20[1] and based on the 7/8 cut-off point used widely in southern Africa). In Durban, nearly half (45%) of the women had a score indicating poor mental health (with a score above the cut-off); in Lusaka, a third (32%) of the women also showed signs of poor mental health. Despite the differences, this indicates a high percentage of women showing symptoms of mental ill-health in Lusaka and Durban, both higher than might have been expected.

In both cases, the question that most women answered in the affirmative was 'Do you feel unhappy?' Nearly 60 per cent of the Durban women and 43 per cent of the Lusaka women said they felt unhappy. Over half (53%) the women in both groups had experienced headaches. More than half (56%) of the Durban women reported sleeping badly, double the rate of the Lusaka women. Twice the percentage of women in Durban had lost interest in things than in Lusaka (40% versus 20%, respectively). Approximately one in seven (15%) women in both cases reported having considered suicide.

The women's self-reported health

While the women in Durban were more likely to report poor mental health, the reverse was found for self-reported health. One in ten women in Lusaka said she

---

1   SRQ20 refers to a 20-question mental health self-reporting questionnaire
         developed by the WHO as a screening instrument validated for use in
         developing countries.

had poor health, compared with one in 25 women in Durban. Self-reported health was found to provide information on particular aspects of health. The spontaneous health problems reported by the women focused on their physical health, with women never revealing indicators of their mental state of health or disclosing that their mental ill-health might be of concern. This confirms the findings of Aidoo and Harpham (2001, p.206) in Lusaka that for many low-income women, only physical symptoms are defined as ill-health and the work of Tijhuis *et al.* (1995, p.1520) in the Netherlands, who notes that 'respondents may view psychiatric problems as personal problems and not as health problems'.

In the focus groups, there was a ready awareness of the way in which emotional, psychological, mental and financial concerns were associated. The women in the focus groups acknowledged the impact of poverty on their mental health. Women reported that the number of women feeling vulnerable is 'ever increasing'. Further, several women expressed concern about access to basic necessities and the lack of alternatives to exploitative work. Chronic poverty in the community has its toll: 'You can help a neighbour and give food for two days; after that they could still not have food. There are people who would tell that four days have passed without food, including the children.'

The close link between poverty and mental ill-health of women emerging from the focus groups was not surprising in view of the findings of others who report on the relationships between women, poverty and common mental disorders in four developing countries (Patel *et al.* 1999). In particular, this was in respect to the expectation that women would provide for others in their roles as both mothers and wives. Although not part of this study, in hindsight it would have been useful to further elicit the explanatory models of the women (Jadhav 2001), not only with respect to their state of (mental) health but also with respect to their understanding of underlying causes of their health problems. The value of exploring the explanatory health models of the respondents would have helped to identify their own conceptions of well being '... to ultimately enable poor people to gain for themselves more of the good life to which they aspire' (Narayan *et al.* 2000, p.43).

All the measures of health were found to be associated. These were self-reported health status and mental health. Respondents who had better physical health had better mental health and were less likely to have reported having had a health problem during the previous two weeks. The inverse relationship was also found: those respondents who reported fair or poor health were more likely to have poorer mental health and to report having had a health problem in the previous two weeks. The odds ratio for someone having poor mental health if they had reported poor or fair health for Durban was 3.4, while for Lusaka it was even greater at 5.5. By implication, those reporting to the health centre in Lusaka, although seldom being diagnosed as being depressed or having some mental health problem, were quite likely to be struggling with feelings of, for example, depression and anxiety. Likewise, in Durban, many of the women presenting at a health centre would also be struggling with depression or anxiety symptoms but likely to be treated for physical health problems, as their mental ill-health would not be picked up by healthcare staff (personal communication). At present, there is limited mental health nursing capacity and a lack of training or counselling skills at a primary level. This is largely a result of the exclusion of mental health concerns from the primary care package in South Africa and Zambia until recently. The treatment of mental ill-health at a primary level would begin to address some of the health problems of women. Although the use of healthcare facilities was not assessed in this study, the high levels of poor mental health in women being treated somatically by the clinic staff has health services implications for policy-makers.

The quantification, descriptions and treatment of ill-health, however, can only go so far. Just as important is understanding the underlying causes of ill-health. In reflecting on community psychiatry in both London and Bangalore, Jadhav (2001) suggests that a 'common failure is the inadequacy of professional formulations that fail to give due regard to social, economic and political problems such as poverty and dispossession'. A balance is needed between the treatment of ill-health through the biomedical approach and addressing the underlying development challenges as a broad preventive health promotion strategy. It is within this lacuna that the question of the association between mental health and social capital emerges.

Social capital and health
Group membership and health
The groups that the women participated in were almost entirely church groups that performed social support functions. These groups could be described as contributing to social support (as cognitive social capital) but did not seem to offer opportunities for accessing resources or getting ahead. In Durban, the high levels of unemployment, lack of local income-generating opportunities, absence of facilities and limited range of community activities all impact on women's health indirectly through poverty. These factors and the marginal trust between neighbours and partners further impact on the mental health of women. A sense of belonging in the community ('Do you feel part of the neighbourhood?') had a direct impact on the mental health of women. A number of social capital components were associated with the mental health of the women indirectly through 'a sense of belonging'. While the women of the settlement in Durban would be described as having limited bridging capital, when assessed in terms of

their involvement in supportive groups, the limited social capital that they had could be described as bonding capital. It may be that in cases of extreme poverty and social stress, opportunities for building bonding capital form a first step towards the realization of structural capital, which will help women ultimately to move from getting by to getting ahead.

In Lusaka, involvement with the church (being a member of a church group) was associated with better health. Being a member of a group was found to be associated with both better self-reported health and better mental health. Those who were members of a group had a mean SRQ score of lower than the overall study mean of 5.6 compared with those who were not members of a group, for whom the SRQ mean was 7.9. Given the finding from the statistical analysis that positive self-reported health and mental health were associated with group membership, it is not surprising that there were numerous focus group references to the role that membership of a church group played in the lives of women. One woman said: 'Most women are participating in church groupings. The church was very active and helpful in the area especially to those who were very vulnerable like the widows and orphans.'

Church support was also found to be important at times of crises: 'Church participation had a lot to offer especially during calamities like death of a family member, unable to pay back micro-credit to micro-credit organizations, lack of food, lack of clothes and lack of family support.'

For some women, the church performed a unique caring role: 'The only [group] membership which could help women was that of church groupings.'

One of the additional roles performed by the church appeared to include access to information: 'Those who struggled could be assisted by church groupings giving them enough information about where and how to access micro-credit and jobs.'

Clearly, the church performs an important role in supporting women and in helping them cope with difficulties in their daily lives. Key roles identified in the focus group discussions include access to sources of information, accessing jobs and micro-credit, financial help, help during bereavement, emotional support, group support, etc.

While the quantitative and qualitative results of this study point to the important role of churches in both the mental and self-rated health of the women, the specific relationships between aspects of health outcomes and specific roles played by the church would need to be the subject of further detailed data collection and analysis. Nevertheless, it would appear from a social capital perspective that church groups play an important role in helping women to bond within their community, to adapt and to cope better. In this study, there was very limited evidence that membership of a church group helped women to get ahead (bridging capital). Good health, steady income and strong family support were the key factors identified by the women of the settlements in Lusaka as key to reducing women's vulnerability. Factors that impacted on women's mental health negatively included an absence of these factors and having someone in the household who had been ill for a long period of time.

Group membership provided an important resource for women who were members of a church group. These groups provided social support and a strong socializing function. There was a limited range of other groups that women belonged to. Nevertheless, women were aware of the opportunities of income-generating groups and yet, due to their financial and social circumstances, participating in these types of groups was almost entirely beyond their reach.

This summary highlights the important role played by cognitive social capital in sustaining the health of women. In particular, attention is drawn to the ways in which the health of women is impacted on by the church and social support from other sources. The analysis has, however, also highlighted the very limited extent to which women in Lusaka are getting ahead due to their economic and political marginalization.

Discussion

The findings may be considered to indicate that women's activities in church groups and social support provided social capital that improved their self-rated mental and physical health. Participating in church groups and having social support could be described as resources that help women to get by and contributed to their sense of belonging. Very few women had ever participated in civic activities, other than voting in South Africa. Despite their very different sociopolitical histories, the women in both settlements felt as if they had minimal power to influence decisions in their community. Women expressed that they felt they were largely excluded from participating in civic activities, in part due to their own experience of being token participants and finding that their views were not heard. While seeing the need to participate in activities that would help them get ahead, women very seldom took part in civic actions, community-focused groups or income-generating activities that would facilitate mutually beneficial collective action. The findings are not surprising. In a context of deep poverty and gender disempowerment, the women in both the Durban and the Lusaka case studies focused their attention on meeting their basic needs. In such contexts, cognitive social capital necessary for 'getting by' remains their primary focus. The high level of depression among the women is understandable in view of their lack of opportunities. Further, the findings point to the importance of churches in sustaining the health of women in the short and medium term and of focusing on addressing poverty and underdevelopment in the medium and longer term.

Research in Johannesburg found that in low-income communities, the dominant type of association is one that meets survival needs and does not manifest a commitment to engaging in community activities (White *et al.* 1995, p.43). This is very different from the wide-ranging civic roles performed by groups in Italy or the USA described by Putnam (2000, p.345). Harrison (2001, p.7), also working in Johannesburg, suggests that 'what is needed for realizing and pursuing social capital as a development resource is determining what is required to develop relationships between the state and civil domain'. Given the deep poverty in both communities and the struggle women have in getting by, it would appear that the social capital women have access to merely helps them to get by and is a far cry from the more developmental opportunities of social capital at a community level.

The findings point to the need to address the underlying structural inequalities, such as poverty and gender inequality, which limit the capacity of women to live up to their full potential. This is beyond the direct scope of the health system but fundamental to social justice and a rights approach to health and development. There is, however, an important immediate role for the primary health system in responding to women's mental health in low-income communities. This role is to recognize the fundamental contribution of mental health in women's overall health and to provide appropriate treatment. The response of the health system would need to be through programmes such as counselling, support groups and other community mental health initiatives in addition to making medication available. The response of the health sector would need to be complemented by other strategies. Existing support systems helping women, such as friends, family, church and other groups, should be reinforced and encouraged to develop further. A holistic approach to the development of low-income communities is needed in order to provide women with access to opportunities that help women get by better and to get ahead through targeted empowerment, microcredit and support group programmes.

However, the study, which focused on women, also raises a number of questions about community social capital and gender dynamics, including: How does the social capital of men living in these contexts differ from that of women? In particular, do men have access to more structural social capital as a resource? What is the relationship between the mental health of men and their social capital? How would empowerment initiatives targeting women impact on the gender power relations, social capital and mental health of women in these contexts?

There is no question that the relationship between social capital and mental health is complex and multidimensional. In a context of developing countries characterized by poverty, gender inequalities and poor health, the interface of social capital and mental health may provide a yet to be understood opportunity for intervention in the social determinants of health terrain.

References

Aidoo, M. (1998) Explanations for the causes of mental ill-health among low-income women in an urban area: the case of Zambia. Unpublished PhD thesis. London: South Bank University.

Aidoo, M., Harpham, T. (2001) Explanatory models of mental health problems: comparison of low-income women and health care practitioners in Lusaka, Zambia. *Health Policy and Planning 16*, 206–213.

Bain, K., Hicks, N. (1998) Building social capital and reaching out to excluded groups: the challenge of partnerships. Presented for the CELAM meeting The Struggle Against Poverty: Towards and Turn of the Millennium. 21 April 1998. Washington, DC: The World Bank.

Beall, J. (2000) Valuing social resources or capitalizing on them? Limits to pro-poor urban governance in nine cities of the south. Urban Governance, Partnership and Poverty Working Paper 19. Birmingham: International Development Department, University of Birmingham.

Cross, C., Bekker, S., Clark, C. (1992) *Fresh Starts: Migration Streams in the Southern Informal Settlements of the Durban Functional Region.* Pietermaritzburg: Town and Regional Planning Commission.

Fine, B. (2001) *Social Capital vs. Social Theory: Political Economy and Social Science at the Turn of the Millennium.* London: Routledge.

Harpham, T., Blue, I. (1995a) Urbanization and mental health in developing countries: an introduction. In T. Harpham and I. Blue (eds) *Urbanization and Mental Health in Developing Countries: An Introduction.* London: Avebury.

Harpham, T., Blue, I. (1995b) *Urbanization and Mental Health in Developing Countries.* London: Avebury.

Harpham, T., Grant, E., Thomas, E. (2002) Measuring social capital within health surveys: some key issues. *Health Policy and Planning 17*, 106–111.

Harrison, K. (2001) Social capital, local government and trust. In S. Parnell, E. Pieterse, M. Swilling and D. Wooldridge (eds) *Developmental Local Government: The South African Experiment.* Cape Town: University of Cape Town Press.

Jadhav, S. (2001) Community psychiatry and clinical anthropology in cultural psychiatry: Euro-international perspectives. In A.T. Yilmaz, M.G. Weiss and A. Reicher-Rossler (eds) *Bibliotheca Psychiatrica.* Basel, Switzerland: Karger.

Krishna, A., Shrader, E. (1999) Social Capital Assessment Tool. Presented at Conference on Social Capital and Poverty Reduction. 22–24 June 1999. Washington, DC: World Bank.

Marmot, M., Wilkinson, R.G. (1999) *Social Determinants of Health.* Oxford: Oxford University Press.

McKenzie, K., Whiteley, R., Weich, S. (2002) Social capital and mental health. *British Journal of Psychiatry 181*, 280–283.

Narayan, D., Waeton, M., Petesch, P. (2000) *Voices of the Poor.* World Bank Washington and Oxford University Press: New York.

Patel, V., Araya, R., de Lima, M., Ludermir, A., Todd, C. (1999) Women, poverty and common mental disorders in four restructuring societies. *Social Science and Medicine 49*, 1461–1471.

Putnam, R. (2000) *Bowling Alone.* New York: Simon and Schuster.

Serageldin, I., Grootaert, C. (2000) Defining social capital: an integrating view. In P. Dasgupta and I. Serageldin (eds) *Social Capital: A Multifaceted Perspective.* Washington, DC: World Bank.

Tijhuis, M.A.R., Flap, H.D., Foets, M., Gronewegen, P.P. (1995) Social support and stressful life events in two dimensions: life events and illness as an event. *Social Science and Medicine* *40*, 1513–1526.

United Nations (2001) Road map towards the implementation of the Millenium Development Goals. 56th session of the UN General Assembly.

Webb, D. (1999) A psychiatric morbidity profile of adults in high HIV/AIDS prevalence areas: the case of Kafue District, Southern Zambia. Unpublished working draft. Harare: Southern African AIDS Information Dissemination Service (SAFAIDS).

White, C., Dlodlo, N., Segooa, W. (1995) *Democratic Societies? Voluntary Association and Democratic Culture in a South African Township.* Johannesburg: Centre for Policy Studies.

Woolcock, M. (1998) Social capital and economic development: towards a theoretical synthesis and policy framework. *Theory and Society 27*, 151–208.

World Health Organization (WHO) (1994) *A User's Guide to the Self-reporting Questionnaire (SRQ).* Geneva: World Health Organization.

World Health Organization (WHO) (2001) Mental health: new understanding, new hope. In *World Health Report, 2001*. Geneva: World Health Organization.

CHAPTER 8

Social capital and youth mental health in Cali, Colombia

Trudy Harpham, Emma Grant and Simon Snoxell

Introduction

This chapter presents a study of a project in Cali, Colombia, that focused on strengthening social capital among youth in order to reduce violence and to improve mental health. It was an unusual project in several ways: the local government's health department abandoned a medical model and adopted a social model to improve the wellbeing of youth; levels of violence were high; strengthening social capital was regarded as a way forward at a very early stage in the debate about social capital and health; there was an opportunity to collect baseline data on all the key variables, which enabled a proper evaluation to be carried out; the municipality identified a local non-governmental organization as the most appropriate institution to implement the intervention; and the evaluation involved Colombian implementers, British evaluators and US funders. Some of these special characteristics raise questions about the generalizability of the project and its results. However, many of the findings may be relevant to other low-income urban settings in which there are high levels of youth violence.

The chapter considers the debate about social capital interventions, presents the setting of Colombia and Cali, and then goes on to describe the methods used, the intervention and the results.

Strengthening social capital: a summary of the debate

It is not clear whether external agencies can intervene effectively in the development of social capital. Some may view state funding of associations as governmental intrusion. Others view the emphasis on social capital as a way of relieving the state of responsibility for poverty reduction. The social capital literature documents a wide range of areas in which social capital has been undermined by government, the private sector and even civil society, with few examples of successful attempts to foster or strengthen social capital (Fukuyama 1995; Gugerty and Kremer 2000). Some authors even argue that 'policies designed simply (simple-mindedly) to strengthen social capital are likely to have some ugly broader effects' (Adler and Kwon 1999, p.14).

Despite the growing complexity and criticism of social capital, both in theory and in practice, a number of authors believe that well-planned policy can encourage social capital formation (Putnam 2004), and some organizations have attempted to integrate social capital into public policy as a useful conceptual tool (the World Bank, Policy Research Initiative Canada, Organization for Economic Cooperation and Development, United Kingdom Social Exclusion Unit). Policy Research Initiative Canada (2003, p.59) usefully outlines four dimensions of a social capital intervention:

- Development or mobilization of social networks, social support structures and local associations.

- Strengthening of ties among existing communities and social institutions/organizations.

- Promotion of civic engagement (volunteering, civic participation).

- Development or access to information channels and links with political or economic power brokers and institutions.

Some authors have called for the social capital debate to move forward from the initial question in terms of opposites – 'intervention' versus 'non-intervention' to the 'where and how to intervene' (van Kemenade *et al.* 2003).

The setting
The country
Colombia is a democratic middle-income country with great disparities of wealth. Its inhabitants have historically suffered from profound insecurity. Since 2002, President Uribe's 'democratic security policy' has aimed to secure territory in the countryside and the cities, while the USA-backed Plan Colombia programme has attempted to reduce coca production through aerial fumigation campaigns targeting peasant farmers with few alternatives available to them. However, the guerrillas (Fuerzas Armadas Revolucionarias de Colombia (FARC) and the Ejército de Liberación Nacional (ELN)) and right-wing paramilitaries continue their armed struggle. Impunity, killing, intimidation, extortion, kidnapping and drug-trafficking continue, and in many areas the civilian population remains exposed to attacks from all armed groups (Colombia Forum 2004). From

2002–04, bomb attacks by illegal armed groups have increasingly been aimed at urban targets, bringing greater insecurity into these areas.

The 2002 report of the World Health Organization (WHO) cites Colombia as having the world's highest homicide rate, at 84 per 100,000 population, although this rate varies considerably between cities and even between neighbourhoods. A high proportion of these murder victims are youths – the focus of this study. It is commonly held that over 80 per cent of Colombia's violent deaths are not related directly to the armed conflict but rather are due to gang and organized crime as well as youth, domestic and neighbour violence. Nevertheless, defining the boundaries between social, economic and political violence is virtually impossible due to the cross-cutting nature of the internal conflict, rooted in economic inequalities and poverty, and the particularly complex role played by narco-trafficking across the different armed groups.

Any study of social capital in Colombia is undertaken in this context of violence. Sudarsky (1999) measured social capital in Colombia as part of the World Values Survey (WVS) and showed that Colombia has some of the world's highest levels of interpersonal distrust and corruption. He found that Colombians have high trust in the church, educational systems, ecological movements and the armed forces; a middle level of trust in the legal system, police and local government; and least trust in parliament, political parties and the guerrillas.

Sudarsky (1999, p.41) ascribes certain negative social characteristics of Colombian society to the absence of social capital:

> From the fundamental comparison of trust in strangers and perceived corruption, Colombia's social capital is feeble. As has been repeated in Mafiosi society, when social capital does not fill society, it is crime, violence and lawlessness that abound. The Colombian society is fractured, atomized, and very few institutions and beliefs contribute to strengthen such an essential resource as social capital.

However, Sudarsky (1999, p.42) goes on to suggest civil society as the key mechanism for addressing this need: 'The message is clear: civil society is the reservoir most important for the generation of social capital and its development through increased membership in secular, non-religious organizations is a clear path to do so.'

The present study considers an intervention that tries to strengthen social capital through such organizations.

The city

Cali is one of the major cities in Colombia, with a population of approximately two million people. The focus of this study is the large, very poor area located on the eastern fringe of the city and known as Aguablanca. This area has a population of around 500,000, a high proportion of which is unemployed. The city, and especially Aguablanca, has high homicide rates. In 2001, Cali's homicide rate was 90 per 100,000 (Social Observatory 2003). Cali's youth are particular victims of this violence. In 2002, 44 per cent of the city's homicide victims were aged between 15 and 25 years (Social Observatory 2003).

Methods
Overall research design
The design of the evaluation of the intervention was repeat cross-sectional, quasi-experimental, with the inclusion of a control commune that did not have the intervention. The study was not longitudinal (i.e. it did not follow up the same individuals) due to financial and time constraints. A baseline survey of 15- to 25-year-olds (1060 cases) measuring social capital, violence and mental health, and focus groups and key informant interviews were undertaken in year one and repeated in year three (1139 cases) after the intervention. All research was conducted in Spanish.

Measuring mental health
Probable cases of common mental disorders (CMDs; sometimes referred to as mental ill-health) were measured by the Self-Reporting Questionnaire 20 items (SRQ20) recommended by the WHO for assessing the prevalence of depression and anxiety at the community level where diagnoses of specific illness are not required (WHO 1994). The instrument, which consists of 20 yes/no questions, was administered by an interviewer, as it was anticipated that literacy rates may be low among some youth. Researchers had previously determined a cut-off point of 7/8 for the SRQ20 in Armero, Colombia (Lima *et al.* 1991). As this cut-off point was validated against the *Diagnostic and Statistical Manual*, 3rd edition (DSM3), the same cut-off point was used in the current study. Although the validation in Armero was in the context of a disaster, the 7/8 cut-off has also emerged in numerous other studies using the SRQ20 among low-income urban populations in Latin America (Harpham *et al.* 2003).

Measuring social capital
The instrument applied in this study is called the Adapted Social Capital Assessment Tool (A-SCAT) and was developed over three years by the research team (see Harpham *et al.* 2002). It draws upon multiple sources: the Social Capital Assessment Tool (developed by the World Bank) (Krishna and Shrader 1999); measures of informal social control as used by Sampson *et al.* (1997); and the Barometer of Social Capital, or BARCAS (Sudarsky 1999) using questions from

the World Values Survey (WVS). Questions covered participation, trust in institutions, thick and thin trust, social cohesion, solidarity and social control. All questions used a recall period of one year and a five-point Likert scale, except the measurement of group participation, which asked whether respondents were active members of a range of prompted organizations, and civic participation of youth, which used a three-point scale.

Measuring violence

The violence measurement tool was adapted from the Actitudes y Normas Culturales frente a Violencia (ACTIVA) questionnaire, previously applied in several cities in Latin America, including Cali (Orpinas 1998). The instrument covers consequences of violence in the neighbourhood and in the family, domestic violence, non-familial violence (categorized into witness, victim and perpetrator), and norms relating to violence (justification of violence as conflict resolution) in the family and neighbourhood. All attitudinal questions used a five-point Likert scale. Behavioural questions used a three-point scale asking whether the action had been undertaken never, done once or done more than once. The recall period was one year, apart from questions about perpetration of violence against children, for which the recall period was reduced to one month.

Sampling

Using a formula for the comparison of two proportions and given the possibility of cluster effects and refusals, a final sample size of 1168 was arrived at by assuming a prevalence of key violence variables of 50 per cent (as is the practice of CISALVA, Violence Research Institute of the University of Valle, Cali), and objectives of a 10 per cent reduction in the incidence of violence and a 30 per cent reduction in perceptions of violence.

Commune 14 was chosen as the non-intervention zone, because of the three communes of Aguablanca it is the most similar to the intervention Commune 13 in size and demography. From designated clusters and randomly selected houses, youths who had lived in the commune for more than a year were approached for interview. The non-response rate was nine per cent in the first phase and two per cent in the second phase.

The social capital intervention

Harpham et al. 2004 suggested that youths have high levels of trust in the church, schools and health centres. Eight-five per cent of youths thought that the church provided a good service to the community. Youths were also found to have high trust in immediate neighbours, friends and family, suggesting strong bonding social capital. For example, 85 per cent said they would leave keys with their neighbours. Perceptions of solidarity and perceptions of civic participation were also generally high: 75 per cent of the sample said that there are neighbours who would take care of their children and 72 per cent said they voted in elections. Perceptions of social cohesion (i.e. feelings of neighbourly unity and mutual respect), trust in the wider community and social control (i.e. willingness for collective action for communal benefit) were found to be of a moderate level. Only 35 per cent of youths trusted the police. Civic and group participation of youths was also low. Only 18 per cent of youths participated in cultural, sports or dance groups, the most popular of the groups listed. The intervention was, therefore, initiated in a context of relatively high bonding social capital, moderate to low bridging and linking capital, and low associational membership. The intervention aimed to draw on and further develop this high bonding social capital in order to build bridging and linking social capital.

The intervention was implemented in 2002–03. Since 1992, the non-governmental organization Fundaps (Consulting Foundation in Health and Social Development Programs) has worked on health issues with the youth in Aguablanca. From 1999, Fundaps has concentrated more specifically on the issue of violence.

Social capital was used both as the conceptual tool for designing the project and as the central means of realizing the project's long-term goal: to reduce violence levels and to improve mental health. Social capital was defined as including both structural (associations, civic participation, etc.) and cognitive (norms, attitudes, trust) components. The intervention aimed to influence all four of the dimensions of social capital listed by Policy Research Initiative Canada.

The intervention promoted peaceful coexistence by explicitly building structural youth social capital by drawing on close bonds between group members to strengthen community social connectedness, using health centres as a focus for violence-related activities and linking youths to state institutions. Youth group activities also aimed to promote wider cognitive social capital within the community, such as mutual trust and solidarity. Key to these aims was to develop greater youth civic engagement; improved youth leadership and conflict-resolution skills; youth willingness to dialogue with and greater trust in institutions through the promotion of new communication channels; greater recognition by government of the experiences and energy of young people; the creation of new services and programmes oriented to youth development and peaceful coexistence; and institutional and policy coordination at the municipal level.

The intervention worked through seven youth groups that were at least seven years old. Most members are Afro-Colombian, divided equally between men and women, ranging from 15 to 27 years. Only one group is composed exclusively of women. Most of the members have completed high school and live with their parents, even though some of them are parents themselves. These groups specialized in areas such as sex education, environmental projects, healthcare, income-generation, participation, folklore, dance and sport.

The groups suffered from a high turnover of members and internal conflicts. Although youth groups were recognized legally, they could not fulfil their legal and accounting responsibilities. It was, therefore, difficult to establish contracts and manage financial resources. Several groups had experience working with local municipal bodies (health centres, Casa de Justicia) and city departments. However, their efforts were limited, occasionally incomplete and informal. The groups often lost momentum and motivation.

Workshops and meetings were undertaken with Fundaps in 2001, where it was agreed that groups rather than individuals should be responsible for negotiating with institutions in order to develop proper legal arrangements with partners and activities that encourage wider participation, reflect community interests and build peaceful coexistence. In 2002, Fundaps ran capacity-building courses, including organizational development, negotiation skills, planning techniques, accounting, leadership, documentation and information technology.

Eleven projects were carried out in 2003 in cooperation with the Casa de Justicia, health services and other city departments. Funding sources included Fundaps, the Municipal Health Department, the Municipal Department responsible for security, Catholic Organisation for Relief and Development (CORDAID) of the Netherlands and US Agency for International Development (USAID) of the USA. Individual project budgets ranged from US$3500 to US$30,000. Technical assistance to groups included at least two counselling and monitoring sessions per week. Projects targeted a wide range of beneficiaries, including youth leaders, youth groups, parents, health volunteers and children. Projects generated greater participation in promoting health and community development, strengthened administrative capacities, tackled drug addiction and promoted alternative conflict-resolution mechanisms. Sociocultural projects promoted peaceful coexistence through folklore, hip-hop music and theatre.

As part of the aim of improving inter-institutional policy coordination, Fundaps played a key role in founding the Peaceful Coexistence Committee in 2003. This committee is composed of one youth group representative and directors and representatives of local and city institutions. The committee is responsible for promoting institutional exchanges, formulating peaceful coexistence policies, evaluating and approving project proposals, and managing grants. The Fundaps intervention forms part of a wider municipal violence-prevention programme known as Districts of Peace. This provides an alternative to repressive anti-violence policies.

Results

Prevalence of mental health at baseline and its associations

The prevalence of CMDs at baseline across the whole sample was 24 per cent (with no difference between the intervention and control communities). This prevalence is high compared with other low-income, mixed-sex, mixed-age urban populations in developing countries (Harpham et al. 2003). In order to understand the factors associated with CMDs, regressions were undertaken that used CMD caseness as the dependent variable and social capital, violence and demographics as independent variables. Social capital and violence variables had been reduced through factor analysis. For full details of the regressions, see Harpham et al. (2005). When only demographic factors were entered into the model, being a woman, having a low education and working in the informal sector were the main risk factors for CMDs. When social capital factors were added into the model, coming from outside Cali and living in inadequate housing entered the model as risk factors. People who had high levels of thin trust (trust spread thinly across a wide range of people, as opposed to thick trust, which refers to a concentration of trust among a few people) were less likely to suffer from mental health problems. Sociodemographic risk factors remained the same as in the first model. When violence factors were added, housing quality and thin trust (the only significant social capital factor) dropped out. Being a woman, having a low education, earning a living in the informal sector and being a migrant remained as risk factors. Three violence risk factors entered: being a victim of neighbourhood violence, experiencing violence in the family, and suffering the consequences of violence.

The pattern of these associations suggests that any interventions that do manage to strengthen youth social capital may be unlikely to affect levels of mental health directly. Gender-specific policies (protecting the mental health of young women), poverty-reduction policies (increasing education and employment in the formal sector) and violence reduction emerge as the actions more likely to influence mental health. (Although, of course, these cross-sectional data can say nothing about causal directions – it might be that people with mental ill-health are dropping out of education, are not getting formal employment and are more likely to feel the effects of violence.) However, there remained some hope that the social capital intervention might make a difference to mental health, because it was discovered that several social capital factors were associated with violence. In particular, high levels of cognitive social capital (trust, perceptions of solidarity and cohesion, etc.) were associated with low levels of witnessing violence, being a victim of violence, perpetrating violence or suffering the consequences of violence. Surprisingly, high levels of structural social capital (membership, associational life, etc.) were associated with high levels of violence. This might be related to the negative social capital type of story (gangs, etc.), or it might be that higher levels of exposure to the streets and community life are related to higher levels of exposure to violence. Possibly, being exposed to high levels of violence might lead youths to take civic action or to seek out group structures where they feel safer.

On reflection of these results, the implicit hypothesis became more long-term and less direct: if the intervention managed to increase social capital, that might reduce violence, which might in turn reduce mental ill-health.

After the intervention

At the follow-up survey, the prevalence of CMDs was the same in both communities. Levels of social capital remained broadly the same in the intervention commune, while they decreased in the non-intervention commune. Levels of violence remained high in both communes. The intervention may have had a protective influence on levels of social capital in a context of very high violence but has not yet had an impact on violence or mental health. The intervention continues, and it was perhaps asking a lot to find evidence of impact within a couple of years. A further survey in a year or so might yield more positive results.

Discussion

> There remains a need to further increase understanding of the critical factors and influences which contribute to young people's mental health.
>
> (Donald *et al.* 2000, p.2)

The need to focus on youth mental health in developing countries and the curiosity as to whether social capital can (i) be strengthened by outside agencies and (ii) have an impact on mental health makes this study particularly interesting. The fact that an explicitly social model was used to improve the health and wellbeing of youths is noteworthy in itself. The fact that only two communities (one intervention, one control) were involved precluded an examination of social capital at the ecological level, and all analyses were at the individual level. Also, because the study was repeat cross-sectional and not longitudinal, it was not possible to examine whether those individuals who perceived their social capital to have been strengthened had improved mental health. However, the indications that social capital levels were protected in the intervention community suggest that it may indeed be possible to strengthen social capital exogenously. And if the mental health of the youth in the intervention community is measured again in a couple of years, we may find that their mental health has improved. We should note, nevertheless, that the external and uncontrollable factors, such as the changing political context, make it harder to measure significant change or to necessarily attribute it to one programme or another. In a country such as Colombia, policies such as the military Democratic Security Policy and related civilian informer networks are highly likely to impact directly on the civilian population, undermining levels of trust and social cohesion and overriding any gradual change that might be attributed to the intervention. Thus, in many ways, the odds are stacked against the research finding significant change. Bearing such caveats in mind, it is nevertheless concluded that strengthening social capital in these types of environments is possible and that further research is needed in order to assess any impact on mental health. We need to progress from studies that merely describe the relationship between social capital and mental health towards intervention studies that address the question 'What makes a difference?'

Acknowledgements

The US National Institutes of Health funded this research, and the authors are grateful to Dr Carlos Rodriguez, the Director of Fundaps, the implementing NGO, for his partnership throughout the project.

References

Adler, P., Kwon, S.W. (1999) Social capital: the good, the bad and the ugly. Paper presented at the 1999 Academy of Management meeting, August, Chicago.

Colombia Forum (2004) Issue 36. Analytical bulletin distributed by ABColombia Group, London. See www.usofficeoncolombia.org/coloforum/cf36.pdf.

Donald, M., Dower, J., Lucke, J., et al. (2000) The Queensland Young People's Mental Health Survey Report. Brisbane: Centre for Primary Health Care, School of Population Health, and Department of Psychiatry, University of Queensland.

Fukuyama, F. (1995) Social capital and the global economy. Foreign Affairs 74, 89–103.

Gugerty, M., Kremer, M. (2000) Does development assistance help build social capital? Social Capital Initiative working paper no. 20. Washington, DC: World Bank.

Harpham, T., Grant, E., Thomas, E. (2002) Measuring social capital within health surveys: key issues. Health Policy and Planning 17, 106–111.

Harpham, T., Reichenheim, M., Oser, R., et al. (2003) Measuring mental health in a cost-effective manner. Health Policy and Planning 18, 344–349.

Harpham, T., Grant, E., Rodriguez, C. (2004) Mental health and social capital in Cali, Colombia. Social Science and Medicine 58, 2267–2278.

Harpham, T., Snoxell, S., Grant, E., Rodriguez, C. (2005) Mental health of youth in Cali, Colombia. British Journal of Psychiatry 187, 161–167.

Krishna, A., Shrader, E. (1999) Social Capital Assessment Tool. Washington, DC: World Bank.

Lima, B., Pai, S., Santacruz, H., Lozano, J. (1991) Psychiatric disorders among poor victims following a major disaster – Armero, Colombia. Journal of Nervous and Mental Disease 179, 420–427.

Orpinas, P. (1999) Who is violent? Factors associated with aggressive behaviors in Latin America and Spain. *Revista Panamericana de la Salud Publica 5*, 232–244.

Policy Research Initiative Canada (2003) Social Capital as a Public Policy Tool. Social capital workshop, June 2003. Ottawa: Policy Research Initiative Canada.

Putnam, R. (2004) Commentary: 'health by association' – some comments. *International Journal of Epidemiology 33*, 1–4.

Sampson, R., Raudenbusch, S., Earls, F. (1997) Neighbourhoods and violent crime: a multi-level study of collective efficacy. *Science 277*, 918–924.

Social Observatory, Municipality of Cali, Colombia (2003) *Report: First Semester of 2003 in Cali*. Cali: Municipality of Cali.

Sudarsky, J. (1999) Colombia's social capital: the national measurement with the BARCAS. Unpublished. See www.worldbank.org/poverty/scapital/library/sudarsky.htm

van Kemenade, S., Paradis, S., Jenkins, E. (2003) Can Public Policy Address Social Capital? Social Capital as a Public Policy Tool. Ottawa: Policy Research Initiative Canada. http://policyresearch.gc.ca/page.asp?pagenm=v6n3_art_07 (accessed 1 August 2004).

World Health Organization (WHO) (1994) *A User's Guide to the Self Reporting Questionnaire (SRQ)*. Geneva: World Health Organization.